THE ART OF SON

MW00808150

To Cindy + Rubin! I pray this book is a blessing.

WHICH SON WILL YOU BE?

ISRAEL DAVID CAMPBELL

The Art of Sonship
King David Had 20 Sons - Only One Truly Reigned. Which Son Will You Be?

Copyright © 2018 by Israel Campbell

First Edition, 2018
ISBN: 978-1-94716-577-9

CONTENTS

ENDORSEMENTS

It's not common to find a resource with such a helpful balance of both biblical revelation and practical application. My good friend Israel Campbell has been living for decades what he teaches in this book. I believe that very few are able to address this subject with as much wisdom and compassion as he does. Get ready to be equipped and encouraged to strengthen the "father" and "son" relationships in your life so you can walk in the purpose and calling you were destined for!

Jason Bolin
Seven Springs Church, Powder Springs, GA

Which son will you be? Wow, what a question! The concept that sonship isn't limited by our natural bloodline but spiritual DNA is life changing! We are not a product of our genetics or circumstances but we can actually choose this heavenly adoption. No matter what your experiences are with natural fathers or spiritual fathers you can choose to be a son/daughter that walks in purpose, destiny and has an inheritance in Christ Jesus. Israel Campbell is uniquely qualified to speak into these issues and brings unmatched experience with incredible insights that will bring revelation and healing in every chapter. The body of Christ needs this book!

Landon Schott
The Rev Ministries & Mercy Culture Church

The carefully crafted words of Truth in *The Art of Sonship* will open up God's plan and purpose for you as a spiritual son or daughter. If you have ever struggled with the question of destiny and how to move beyond "father wounds" or a painful past, you will find fresh hope and new direction in these pages. Israel Campbell powerfully unpacks the stories of King David and his sons to instruct us, guide us, and teach us how to be spiritual sons and daughters that thrive.

Gregory L. Jantz, PhD, C.E.D.S.
Founder, The Center - A Place of HOPE

It's no secret that the concept of sonship has been distorted and rejected. When I look around today, I see too many striving "Kings" who have yet to first master how to be a true son. I believe this is one of the most important subjects for every generation to learn. Israel has a unique level of authority to speak to what true sonship really looks like, shown in the powerful and inspiring examples from his own life in *The Art of Sonship*.

Josh Kelly
Pastor, Wavechurch (Great Neck Campus), Virginia Beach, VA

ACKNOWLEDGEMENTS

This book could not have been written without the influence of these great spiritual fathers on my life, my ministry, and my relationship with Jesus:

Victor Campbell, Casey Treat, Steve Murray, Mel Bailey, Vince Schott, Tim Bagwell, Clint Brown, John Bevere, Chris Hill, Bishop Bolin, Gerard Keehan, and my pastor, Steve Kelly.

Thank you for the high price you have paid for the next generation to go deeper in relationship to Christ and to do even greater things for the Kingdom of God.

I want to thank my mother, Ruth Graber, who had to be both a mother and a father to me after the death of my dad. During the most difficult years of my life, she loved and supported me…and relentlessly prayed this prodigal son back into the Kingdom.

I also want to thank my wife Rachel, who has been my best friend for over 20 years. She has helped me process and choose the concept of "sonship" in the real world when it wasn't always the easiest choice. I love doing life, ministry, and family with you…what an adventure!

I am so grateful for my children: Phoebe, Chloe, and Silas. My prayer is that you will build on the foundations of your mom and dad, and have a greater influence on the world for Jesus. We've had the privilege to minister around the globe because of the sacrifices made and seeds sown by our own parents. We pray that you go even further than the generations before you!

To my editor, Kelsey Yarnell, thank you for tolerating my abusive use of the English language and helping *The Art of Sonship* become a book that is hopefully read by more people than just my mother!

PREFACE

Will you be a child of promise and destiny, or will you be a child of curse and tragedy?

The Bible is full of stories of sons and daughters who had to answer this question. In The Art of Sonship, *I'll take you through the Biblical accounts of King David's sons, how they responded to this critical choice, and how that response impacted their destinies.*

I'm focusing on the male children of David, but my heart is that this book would speak to daughters too. At its core, sonship is gender-neutral. Just as we are all the Bride of Christ, we are also all sons of God. The principle of sonship and the blessing and value it adds to our lives are available to all who are His children. Throughout Scripture, both men and women, young and old, are all referred to as children of God. "I will be a Father to you, and you shall be my sons and daughters, says the LORD Almighty" (2 Corinthians 6:18).

There are not a lot of topics I feel qualified to write about. There are plenty I'm passionate enough to write down in a journal, but not in a book I want everyone to read.

I know, not exactly the most confident way to kick this thing off, but hang on a minute. Don't walk away. The book you're holding in your hands is not the result of my desire to check an item off my bucket list or my attempt to prove my English teacher wrong.

What you'll find on the following pages flow directly out of my life – this isn't a bunch of ideas…it's my story. My passion. The things I know to be true at the deepest level.

I know what it means to be a son. Obviously, I realize roughly half the population shares this experience with me, but what I'm talking about is bigger than biology.

I'm not one of those people who hears God's audible voice. Most of the time I sense what He is speaking to me and I go with it. But I will never forget the night I heard Him ask me a question that changed my life.

I knew it was God because I wasn't sitting at home by myself quietly waiting for Him to speak to me. I was at a concert – the kind of concert where the decibel levels rival the sound of a jet engine. He's the only One who can talk over that kind of noise. And He did. Out of nowhere, in a single moment, the Holy Spirit brought me back to this notion of *sonship*. He asked me a simple question: "Israel, which son will you be?"

As I began studying this subject I quickly realized God had been asking this same question throughout history.

When God asks, "Which son will you be?" He's not asking you whether or not you're a Christian, a member of His family. The question is, "What kind of Christian will you be?"

The Bible is filled with stories of His children and all of them made a choice. They chose what kind of child they would be. They chose what kind of relationship they would have with their Father. And these choices radically impacted not only their lives, but the lives of their families, their loved ones, their nation and the world.

God hasn't stopped asking the question – He asks it to all of His children, yesterday, today, and tomorrow.

The Bible states that, *"creation waits in eager expectation for the sons of God to be revealed"* (Romans 8:19). Do you realize that all of creation is waiting for you and I to start walking, talking, and acting like true sons of God? I am not talking about adding another "No Jesus, No Peace/Know Jesus, Know Peace" sticker to your collection on the back of your car. I'm not talking about rocking your WWJD bracelet from '98 or stocking up on a fresh supply of "Testamints."

Being religious is not the goal – it never has been. The goal is for God's people to know who they are because they know whose they are.

It's time for the children of God to refuse to settle for anything less than everything God has for them in order to live a life of purpose and destiny.

As we begin this journey together, I'm praying God would speak to you and inspire you to overcome every obstacle in your life in order to enter the fullness of what He has for you. My heart's desire is that you would refuse to settle for anything else.

It's time for you to become a son or a daughter of promise. It is time we learn to master the art of *sonship*.

CHAPTER ONE

A SON TO MANY MEN

For as many as are led by the Spirit of God, these are sons of God.
(ROMANS 8:14, BEREAN LITERAL BIBLE)

Anatomy makes you a male, but it takes something more to be a man. It requires character. And unfortunately, the kind of character I'm talking about is rarely found in males, regardless of culture, location, or era. You might find some men who are intelligent, strong, or compassionate. But I'm talking about the ones who pursue their destiny with integrity, lead others with humility, who rise to the occasion. I'm talking about men of great character- godly men.

All throughout the Bible we see pictures, principles and concepts describing what it means to be a godly man. And one of the foundational characteristics of every godly man is that he understands and values what it means to be a wise and faithful son.

I like to refer to this unique state as biblical *sonship*. It's a subject I'm deeply passionate about. Sonship might sound like an unusual term to you, but I feel God has given me revelation and special insight about this critical issue.

I don't have a PhD in this subject. I haven't logged thousands of hours doing clinical research on relationships between sons and fathers. But one thing about my life is undeniable: I have been a son to many men.

That probably sounds a little strange, so let me explain.

FROM ORPHAN TO BELOVED SON

My biological mother and father had me at a very early age in their lives. Both of them were addicted to drugs, and unfortunately, being pregnant with me didn't give my mother a reason to stop using. When I was born, I went through heroin withdrawals. I spent the first few months of my life in the hospital, being rehabilitated.

These were my earliest experiences of being a son. But I didn't remain the son of my biological parents for very long. Their drug problem only continued to get worse when I was born. By the time I was nine months old, my parents got busted and were sent to jail. They asked a friend to drop me off at my aunt Ruth's house while they were incarcerated, and as a small infant, I was given over to the care of Victor and Ruth Campbell.

At this point you can imagine how the story goes. You've heard it many times before: drug addict parents led to a horrible childhood of abuse, crime and subsequent drug use in the life of the child.

That's not my story. God intervened in my life, and one year after being dropped off at their house as a baby, I officially became the son of my aunt and uncle. The state of California changed my birth certificate and legally I had new parents: two people who related to me as their son, and cared for me as if I was their own.

As a parent, I now realize the incredible temptation my new parents must have wrestled with to protect me from the painful reality of my biological parents. But they chose radical honesty instead. They didn't soften the story – they trusted our love would be strong enough to work through any mistrust or confusion that might result from my birth story. And they were right.

Being adopted never bothered me. I never felt unloved or abandoned or even "second best" because my aunt and uncle cared for me now as mother and father.

Growing up, I was very close to my father Victor. He loved all the time-tested traditions fathers share with their sons. We went fishing, we played football, and we spent wonderful nights together around the campfire under the stars. Not only was he my father and my friend, but he was also my pastor. Victor had gotten radically saved at age 40, and was the pastor of a thriving church in North Seattle, where I grew up.

I'd gone from being an orphan of drug addicts to the beloved son of a godly man.

Our time together was cut short, however, and when I was 16 years old, my father died in a tragic boating accident. Although you probably can't relate to what this was like, I'm sure you can imagine the pain and uncertainty that would fill my life for the next five years. There were no clear answers as to why it happened, or how I could continue to thrive without my father. Growing up is hard enough for a young man, but when your hero, your rock, and your biggest influence disappears in one day, the grief can feel beyond bearable.

I responded by mistreating my mother, and my relationship with God grew more and more distant. I isolated myself from family members and nearly anyone who loved me and tried to care for me.

I felt like I was alone, like not one person in the world understood what I was experiencing. People all around me tried to reach out to help me, including my high school principal, my youth pastor, my sister's husband, my new pastor, even an old guy named Otto who wanted to pursue my now available mother.

During this difficult season, I knew the one person who truly wanted to be my father had been with me all along. He didn't get hauled off to jail and He didn't die in a boat accident. Over and over my heavenly Father came to my side, but each time I rejected His attempts to be with me.

I don't think I was mad at God. I didn't blame Him for the pain I was going through, but I was sick of His Church and most of the people who followed Him. The truth is, I was enjoying my newfound personal space and the freedom that came with little personal accountability.

Eventually, I began to chase the life of a prodigal. Everything that the Church - and my dad - had told me to not to do, I did. I started partying and stealing, and I even got thrown in jail temporarily. And in the process, I gave up on many great friendships. Instead, I chose to spend my time with people who didn't share any of the values my father Victor had instilled in me. I was running from my destiny and for a while, it felt good. It numbed my pain.

But when the music stopped, the lights came on, and the (Party was over) alcohol ran out, I was left alone with my thoughts. I was miserable, and even felt suicidal at times. I'd lost my way, and I was no longer a son.

And then one day, like the young man in Luke 15, I came to my senses and realized that even a life working with pigs would be a huge step up from how I had been living. It all became so clear to me. I knew this one truth more than I'd ever known anything: I needed God.

I needed my heavenly Father to guide me, discipline me, teach me the true value and significance of sonship. Until I truly learned how to be His son, I would never become the man I was destined to be.

In that moment, everything changed, and my life hasn't been the same since. I began attending church again, and to see my God-given talents come to life. I threw myself into ministry and developed relationship with my new senior pastor. This man loved me like a father. He taught me what he knew about being a godly man, kept me accountable, and invested his time and energy in me.

In response, I embraced his leadership, mentorship, and his love for me. I was loyal to him even when I saw his faults, and I was passionate for his vision for seeing the church thrive. Not only did I see him as a father, he treated me as a son.

It was the third time I'd been a son. But this time around was different. Though my pastor was not my father in any traditional sense, he became my father in a different way- as a spiritual father, giving me his time, his counsel, and even his godly affection. He wanted to see me grow into a man of God, a leader, and a future spiritual father myself.

I had become an orphan first, never having an opportunity to know my biological father. Under my adoptive father Victor, I learned what it meant to be "beloved" and what it means to be a godly man. But under my third father - my spiritual father - I learned how to be a man that *chooses* sonship.

THROUGH THE FIRE

I served for years as youth pastor under this spiritual father, and he walked me through some of the most important times of my life. He taught me about marriage, ministry, and how to do life as a godly man and leader. He laid a foundation for me that wouldn't budge, and although I didn't know it at the time, I would continue to know my identity as a son under other spiritual fathers and learn to walk in sonship in every season.

And I thank God for that, because the next few years brought challenges I never could have anticipated—and incredible victories along the way.

My wife and I believe that change is a sacred process, though it is never easy. It wasn't easy to leave behind our community. We loved what God was doing in our church and we were humbled by what God was doing through us as leaders. We loved our pastors and the church God had planted us in. But we knew that God had a change for us, and we knew we needed to obey Him. After praying and seeking counsel from others, my wife and I took a youth pastor position at a thriving church in Orlando, Florida.

Moving to Orlando was a huge stretch for me and Rachel. The culture, location, and ministry style were completely different from what felt familiar to us. It was one of the few seasons in our lives we've wrestled with loneliness. We'd been the golden children at our church in Seattle, and now in Florida, we'd joined an incredibly gifted staff of about 60 people, with over 6,000 church members. Rachel and I aren't exactly introverts – we have big personalities – and yet for a period of time we felt anonymous.

This was a dynamic, growing church with massive momentum. They'd come this far without us, and so we naturally felt like we didn't have anything to bring to the table. Furthermore, we didn't agree with everything going on in the church. There were even situations that we found inappropriate on the leadership level.

But the one thing we couldn't shake was the certainty God had called us there to serve, to lead, and to learn.

Rachel and I refused to quit. We were hungry to learn and we knew God had so much he wanted to teach us in that season. We submitted to His plan, to leadership, and to trust that He was working in us and through us. It was a tough process and there were many times I wanted to leave. But instead, I chose to walk as a son: as one who knows his identity in every season.

Our new senior pastor pushed me to preach with passion, and intentionally put me in uncomfortable situations to help me overcome many of my fears and insecurities. Because of this, I now have the confidence and the ability to effectively preach to a wide variety of ethnic backgrounds and church styles in just about any context in the world. It was an honor to sit under his leadership. This man has impacted the world through his teaching and worship ministry, and he considers me one of his spiritual sons. At the end of our season in Orlando, he launched me to my next season of ministry. He helped me to advance in my calling as a pastor and challenging me to become the man I'm destined to be.

It was the fourth time I'd been a son. And this time, I learned what it meant to *remain* a son even through the fire of uncertainty, loneliness, and temptation to take the easy way out. Ultimately, the influence and guidance of my spiritual father in this season molded me and my wife into leaders capable of thriving in our next roles, as lead pastors of a growing church in North Carolina.

When I became the "boss" as senior pastor, it could have been easy to assume my days of being a son were over. But I'd been through too much to dismiss the importance of remaining a son. Years of experience with the good, the bad, and the ugly would prove again and again that sonship is one one of the primary ways that God loves us, develops us, and promotes us.

Recently God has added another spiritual father to my life – a man with more than 30 years of ministry experience, who has wisdom and leadership that add value to my life on a daily basis. I know the significance of remaining a son to him. I know that in every season of my life, I'll continue to glean from the knowledge and the experience of my spiritual fathers, both past and present.

I'll be a son the rest of my days.

LET'S TALK ABOUT YOU

I may not know your story, but I've heard enough of them to figure out what most of them have in common. Even in the Church, we face pain, heartache and disappointment. I can almost guarantee you that if you haven't yet, you will have times where you feel like you are lost, stuck, or have taken a wrong turn. The question is: what do you do once you're there?

Who has God placed in your life as a spiritual father? How are you investing in that relationship, if at all? Do you know what it means and it takes to be a son?

Given what I have learned, my advice to you is this: learn to be a son, regardless of your particular church, denomination, or leadership. Identify the men you can call spiritual fathers, and develop relationships with them. Know how to build on their foundations as leaders, how to communicate with them, how to remain rooted in your identity as a true son. Know how to overcome bad attitudes and rebellion. Know how to resist pitfalls and temptations. Know how to walk as one who is deeply loved and chosen for a purpose, as Jesus did. Sonship is what will launch you into your destiny.

I guarantee you that you will learn to thrive, to go farther than you ever thought possible, and to remain firmly planted in the house of God through any storms that come your way.

Once a son, always a son.

CHAPTER TWO

ALL CREATION WAITS IN EAGER EXPECTATION

For the anxious longing of the creation waits eagerly for the revealing of the sons of God.

(ROMANS 8:19 NAS)

When my family and I lived in North Carolina, every week I would look forward to trash day. The night before pickup, I would haul large items out onto the sidewalk. I'm talking large boxes, old appliances...I once even put our old couch onto the sidewalk. I would wake up early, peek out the blinds, excited and just a little nervous. Would they pick up the items or leave us with our garbage, to be stuffed into closets, garages, empty drawers?

Every week, without fail, the garbage collectors took anything we put out there and relieved us of our heavy burdens. It was a huge contrast to when we lived in Seattle, where we were stuck with tiny garbage cans and *very* strict rules for trash disposal and recycling (think one bin for paper, one for glass, one for aluminum, and one for compost). We always had too much trash, leaving me to climb the mounds of trash just to try and pack it down. But the garbage system in North Carolina gave us freedom to be a large trash-collecting family. To this day, I still get excited about garbage day.

We all have events in our lives that we get excited for (hopefully, for you it's something more significant than garbage day). Maybe it's a package from Amazon, Dominoe's double-stuffed pizza, Christmas season, tax returns, or your birthday. Sometimes waiting increases anticipation that much more.

The Bible gives us a larger scale picture of something to get excited about. This is bigger and greater than a well-earned vacation or an awesome gift. This is a "revealing" that will affect the whole planet. In Romans 8:19 (NIV) the apostle Paul says,

> *Creation waits in eager expectation for the children of God to be revealed.*

Just like we look forward to certain events because they bring us joy, all of God's created world is also waiting for you and I to become the sons of God.

NATURAL, ETERNAL, AND SPIRITUAL SONSHIP

In order to understand spiritual sonship, it's important that we also understand natural and eternal sonship. Although this book will primarily focus on spiritual sonship, all three types of sonship affect and impact each other.

1. *Natural* sonship is the relationship we have with our natural or biological fathers.
2. *Eternal* sonship is the relationship we have with our Father God, made possible by the death and resurrection of Jesus.
3. *Spiritual* sonship is the relationship or relationships with the men who mentor us, give us counsel, and keep us accountable in our walk with Christ.

Natural sonship

Our experience with natural sonship can affect our experiences of eternal and spiritual sonship. Many of us actually have "daddy issues" that can skew our perspectives of God. For example, if we view our natural fathers as harsh or critical, we might have trouble believing that God is truly good, merciful, and loving because that is not what we have experienced with our biological dads. We might also carry these wounds into our relationships with our spiritual fathers, preventing us from developing close relationships with those that want to mentor and guide us.

It's key that we renew our perspectives and get healing from any pain our natural fathers may have caused us, so that we can to take hold of all that God has for us.

Eternal sonship

One of the keys to the moment of "revealing" described in Romans 8:19 is that we know how to identify as and behave as His sons.

If we don't know our true identities as the sons of God, and His nature as our perfect Father, we won't know that we can go boldly into His presence. We won't know that we have eternal access to God's love, guidance, and acceptance.

Hebrews 10:19 says,

We can boldly enter heaven's Most Holy Place because of the blood of Jesus.

Personally, I don't want to wait until I get to heaven to master this dynamic. We have to get this right, because all of creation is waiting for us to get it right!

Spiritual sonship

I've been to some amazing church conferences all around the world, packed with some of the most influential worship, prophetic preaching and teaching, and practical church growth strategies out there. I've learned a lot from these conferences, but not one (many) emphasized or taught on the power and importance of spiritual sonship.

In the same way that God has destined and purposed us to know Him as Father and ourselves as His children, He has designed us to relate to one another as spiritual sons and spiritual fathers.

Spiritual sonship includes the heart, attitude, and actions taken by a man who wants discipleship, training, and guidance from a spiritual father. Spiritual fathers are the men who can point us where we want to go in our own lives because they have been there themselves.

SPIRITUAL SONSHIP IN THE BIBLE

Spiritual sonship was not invented by the contemporary Church for young men in need of mentorship. Spiritual sonship has Biblical precedent. Throughout Scripture, we see many examples of relationships between spiritual fathers and spiritual sons:

Elisha and Elijah

As they were walking along and talking, suddenly a chariot of fire appeared, drawn by horses of fire. It drove between the two men, separating them, and Elijah was carried by a whirlwind into heaven. Elisha saw it and cried out, "My father! My father! I see the chariots and charioteers of Israel!" And as they disappeared from sight, Elisha tore his clothes in distress.

Elisha picked up Elijah's cloak, which had fallen when he was taken up. Then Elisha returned to the bank of the Jordan River.

(2 Kings 2:11-13)

Elisha was not Elijah's biological son, but he learned how to be a spiritual son from this incredible prophet. Just as Elijah had done, Elisha performed supernatural miracles. But his power and anointing were influenced by coming under the mentorship and leadership of a spiritual father.

Joshua and Moses

Joshua son of Nun, who had been Moses' assistant since his youth, protested, "Moses, my master, make them stop!"

(Numbers 11:28)

Now Joshua son of Nun was full of the spirit of wisdom, for Moses had laid his hands on him. So the people of Israel obeyed him, doing just as the Lord had commanded Moses.

(Deuteronomy 34:9)

Joshua was the natural son of Nun and the spiritual son of Moses. Joshua was one of Moses' chosen men who had served him as a spiritual son, receiving impartation and guidance from this incredible leader. After the death of Moses, Joshua went on to lead the Israelites into the Promised Land, fulfilling the original mission of his spiritual father. Through serving a great leader, Joshua became one of the heroes of the Old Testament.

Timothy and Paul

To Timothy, a true son in the faith:

Grace, mercy, and peace from God our Father and Jesus Christ our Lord.

(1 Timothy 1:1 NKJV)

From our limited perspective as readers of the New Testament, the apostle Paul did not have any natural sons. But Timothy was "a true son" to him, as he was discipled and instructed by this giant in the faith. Paul took a personal interest in the welfare and spiritual growth of this young man, investing his time and energy in Timothy's development.

Elijah, Moses, and Paul were not the biological fathers of Elisha, Joshua, and Timothy. They hadn't changed their diapers, named them, or passed on their genetic DNA. What they were able to impart to these young men was their spiritual DNA: the wisdom, knowledge, and gifts that made them into great men of God (I'll cover this in greater detail in Chapter Four). Elisha, Joshua, and Timothy became incredible spiritual leaders, and in some cases, went farther and accomplished more than their spiritual fathers. Elisha received a double portion of Elijah's spiritual anointing (2 Kings 2:9), Joshua came into possession of the Promise Land (Joshua 1-4), and Timothy led the church of Ephesus, one of the largest and most influential churches in early Church history.

WHAT SONSHIP ISN'T

Now that we know what sonship is according to a biblical perspective, let's talk for a minute about what "sonship" *isn't*.

Unfortunately, the Church hasn't always gotten it right in teaching this concept. Back in the 70's through the 90's, our nation was experiencing a massive cultural revolution characterized by changes in sexual morality, drug usage, multiple wars, and a growth in economic greed. During this time, a new discipleship culture referred to as the "shepherding" movement emerged, helping the Church grow in guidance and direction during this uncertain climate.

Unfortunately, even well-intended "shepherding" in the name of discipleship sometimes turned into spiritual manipulation. Instead of developing true sons and disciples, some leaders attempted to control, rather than guide, Christians. The result was an unhealthy expectation that people could not make any decisions without their spiritual leaders' approval.

True sonship is marked by freedom of choice and empowerment to go further than the previous generation. Because of these past unhealthy spiritual dynamics in the Church, we have a missing generation of sons in the Kingdom of God. Some sons who really wanted to learn, serve, and take up the mantle of spiritual anointing were hurt by being manipulated and controlled by their leaders. As a result, some started their own ministries out of frustration, or fizzled out completely and aren't even in churches today.

Creation is not waiting for division, hurt, and unforgiveness between sons and fathers. Creation is waiting for sonship marked by unity, love, and humility.

WHY IS CREATION WAITING FOR SONSHIP?

Given these past negative experiences people have had in the Church, there may be some who associate sonship with pain or hurt. But sonship ultimately brings blessing and transformation to us and to those around us.

Sonship is what the world is waiting for.

In today's world, we have technologies that make us more efficient, programs to bring us physical/emotional/spiritual transformation, and incredible leadership gurus, and yet our hearts and agenda are more divided than ever before. Without authentic relationships and healthy heart attitudes, we're left isolated, stressed out, and unfulfilled-even in the church. We live in a world desperate for answers. How do we break out of vicious cycles? How do we see real, lasting change in our lives? How do we fulfill our destinies?

I believe sonship is a big part of the answer, because it is both Scripturally-mandated and Kingdom-minded.

Sonship goes completely against the very dog-eat-dog, post-modern thinking style of "Do whatever you feel like doing." The world tells us to do what it takes to stay on top. But the Bible tells us to humble ourselves, serve others, and honor our parents.

And ultimately, there is blessing in obeying the Word of God and not the word of the world.

Being an authentic spiritual son takes the posture of serving and learning from spiritual fathers in order to step into purpose and advance the Kingdom of God. Sonship isn't easy. It's not for the faint of heart. Sonship takes humility and it takes submission. But if we don't learn to walk as sons, we will continue the vicious cycle of living in dysfunctional relationships and stunted destinies. We will miss out on what all creation is waiting for.

God has given us dreams and desires to fulfill, and I believe that sonship is a crucial part of getting there. Sonship empowers the next generation to fulfill the promises of God and see His Kingdom advance on earth.

In 1 Kings 6, we see King Solomon building a temple and completing a task originally given to his father David.

The Temple that King Solomon built for the Lord was 90 feet long, 30 feet wide, and 45 feet high. The entry room at the front of the Temple was 30 feet wide, running across the entire width of the Temple. It projected outward 15 feet from the front of the Temple. Solomon also made narrow recessed windows throughout the Temple.

He built a complex of rooms against the outer walls of the Temple, all the way around the sides and rear of the building. The complex was three stories high, the bottom floor being 7 1/2 feet wide, the second floor 9 feet wide, and the top floor 10 1/2 feet wide. The rooms were connected to the walls of the Temple by beams resting on ledges built out from the wall. So the beams were not inserted into the walls themselves. The stones used in the construction of the Temple were finished at the quarry, so there was no sound of hammer, ax, or any other iron tool at the building site. The entrance to the bottom floor was on the south side of the Temple. There were winding stairs going up to the second floor, and another flight of stairs between the second and third floors. After completing the Temple structure, Solomon put in a ceiling made of cedar beams and planks. As already stated, he built a complex of rooms along the sides of the building, attached to the Temple walls by cedar timbers. Each story of the complex was 7 1/2 feet high.

Then the Lord gave this message to Solomon: "Concerning this Temple you are building, if you keep all my decrees and regulations and obey all my commands, I will fulfill through you the promise I made to your father, David. I will live among the Israelites and will never abandon my people Israel."

(1 Kings 6: 2-13)

Solomon was able to build the temple because his father David already had the plans and the finances saved to accomplish the task. If Solomon had ignored his father or squandered his inheritance, he could have missed the mission completely. He didn't have to start from scratch. His father had already laid the foundations for him. Solomon just followed in his footsteps and built perhaps the greatest and most valuable temple in human history. By today's standards, it would have cost over 216 billion dollars for the gold and silver alone used in this extraordinary piece of architecture.*

Think about it. Yes, we could strive to build our own temples (or businesses or ministries) without the help and guidance of great leaders who have gone before us. Or through sonship, we can serve and learn from great men of God and build on their experiences and their victories. Like Solomon, we can do things that have never been done before for the Kingdom of God. We should desire to go above and beyond our fathers in influencing culture, seeing salvations, and glorifying God in entirely new ways.

THE 10 KEY CHARACTERISTICS OF TRUE SONSHIP

Sonship is a process. It takes courage, perseverance, and great faith. Regardless of where you are on the journey, it's important to pay attention to the key characteristics that can make us good sons.

Here are 10 features that mark the attitude, behavior, and character of true sonship. These are the traits that mark sons who will walk in the fullness of their destiny as they build on the work of their spiritual fathers before them.

1. True sonship starts with having a heart that submits to leadership even when our flesh resists.

2. True sonship is more concerned about creating generational legacy than having five minutes of fame or collecting social media followers.

3. Sonship builds on foundations already put into place by spiritual fathers. True sons make a choice to not tear down what's been built to replace it with their own ministry or vision.

4. True sons make choices to honor others.

5. True sons realize anyone can rationalize their decisions, but choose not to move forward without seeking their spiritual father's blessing.

6. Sonship may change methods, but not the message. True sons don't get frustrated with stale or ineffective methods of ministry— they adapt them or change them.

7. True sons don't get offended with their spiritual fathers' faults and idiosyncrasies. They realize all men of God are just that—men with faults and flaws.

8. Sonship is marked by humility. They realize that the platforms they currently have were "paid for" by their spiritual fathers with personal sacrifice.

9. True sons make faith-based decisions, not fear-based decisions. They can be bold in their choices because they have received courage from their spiritual fathers.

10. True sons cover and protect their spiritual fathers' weaknesses. They understand that covering brings blessing but criticism and pointing out flaws brings destruction (Genesis 9:23).

These characteristics don't come easily. To see these come alive in your own life, you'll have to submit to God, humble yourselves before others, and even make personal sacrifices. But they are guaranteed to bring blessing and produce fruit.

ARE YOU WALKING AS A SPIRITUAL SON?

Now it's time to take stock of your own life. No shame, no discouragement. Just an honest assessment of your identity and where you stand as a spiritual son. Try asking yourself these questions, or go through them with someone you trust.

How is your relationship with your natural father? Great? Just OK? Non-existent? How does this relationship affect your perspective on spiritual and eternal sonship?

Have you been manipulated or hurt by a spiritual father?

Is there a current spiritual father in your life? If not, is there someone who can step into that role?

In the following chapters, we're going to use Biblical examples to help us navigate our hearts through any healing we may need, and to give us practical tools on how to walk successfully in sonship. It's not always easy being a spiritual son, and if you're struggling in your current relationships or attitude towards leadership, that's okay! My prayer is that this book will help you become everything God has destined you to be by helping us all walk in true sonship.

Before beginning Chapter Three, let's pray:

Prayer:

Father God, I realize that all of creation is waiting for me to walk in spiritual sonship, Holy Spirit, heal me in the areas that need healing, and Jesus forgive me where I have been selfish. I believe you are calling me to be a spiritual son. Help me not to wander from person to person but to find the right spiritual father, to put roots down, and to grow in destiny and purpose.

King Solomon Temple, KNCB.ORG Kingdom Networks Christian Broadcasting (https://www.kncb.org/2015/06/11/King-solomon-temple/)

CHAPTER THREE

CHOOSE YOUR OWN ADVENTURE

When I was in elementary school, I had to read a certain number of books to be able to enjoy a pizza party at the end of the school year. The librarian suggested the *Choose Your Own Adventure* book series to me, and with cheese pizza as an incentive, I picked a few out and immediately got hooked (not unlike watching the first few episodes of the TV series *24*…don't say I didn't warn you). I'd read them on the bus to school, at school, on the bus home, and at home. Every night, I fell asleep reading and "choosing my own adventure."

So, what was so special about this series? The *Choose Your Own Adventure* books give you the opportunity to decide how you want the story to continue. If you're facing down a three-headed monster, you can choose to fight it with a sword or to run for your life. Depending on your choice, you turn to a certain page and continue the story. Your choices lead to a unique ending, so that you are as active in the plot as the author.

Other books bored me, but with the *Choose Your Own Adventure* book series, I had that stomach-churning combo of fear and excitement that came with making my own choices—with choosing who I was going to be, how I was going to act, and how the story would end, whether that was in the jaws of the three-headed monster or slaying it with my sword.

Life is not so different, is it? Our destinies and identities are truly defined by the choices we make. We get to choose the adventure!

Unfortunately, much of the time we allow ourselves to be more defined by our circumstances than by our decisions.

Matthew 5:45b (NIV) says,

He causes his sun to rise on the evil and the good, and sends rain on the righteous and the unrighteous.

The longer I've been around, the more I've seen this Scripture fulfilled. People who look like they have it all together have gone through a storm, or are probably in for a storm. Many of us have experienced some kind of tragedy, hurt, unfair treatment, or betrayal in our lives, leading to difficult circumstances that we never saw coming, like sickness, unemployment, or even divorce. It can be easy during trials to feel we don't have the power to make good decisions—but that's just not true! We always have control over the way we respond, and what we will stand for in any given situation.

In the same way that we can experience unexpected difficulties, we can experience unexpected blessings or prosperity that also lead to our circumstances defining us. Instead of intentionally choosing to become people of character, we can get complacent and lazy in our decision making. Everything is already going well—why bother choosing character, integrity, and personal sacrifice?

We might be in a storm, or we might be enjoying the sunnier side of life. Regardless, we make choices every day and in every situation that will affect our futures.

The Bible is full of the stories of sons "choosing their own adventure." Sons like Cain and Abel, or Ham, Shem, and Japheth may not have always been able to control their circumstances, but they could control how they responded to their circumstances. And how they responded ultimately determined their destinies. When they responded in a godly way, they experienced blessing and benefit. But when they didn't choose the right response, they wrecked their futures and came to bad endings.

True sonship really is based on the choices we make, not the circumstances that happen to us.

TWO BROTHERS, ONE DECISIVE CHOICE

The story of the very first sons in history only validates the truth that how we respond to our circumstances determines our destiny.

Now Adam had sexual relations with his wife, Eve, and she became pregnant. When she gave birth to Cain, she said, "With the Lord's help, I have produced a man!" Later she gave birth to his brother and named him Abel.

When they grew up, Abel became a shepherd, while Cain cultivated the ground. When it was time for the harvest, Cain presented some of his crops as a gift to the Lord. Abel also brought a gift—the best portions of the firstborn lambs from his flock. The Lord accepted Abel and his gift, but he did not accept Cain and his gift. This made Cain very angry, and he looked dejected.

"Why are you so angry?" the Lord asked Cain. "Why do you look so dejected? You will be accepted if you do what is right. But if you refuse to do what is right, then watch out! Sin is crouching at the door, eager to control you. But you must subdue it and be its master."

One day Cain suggested to his brother, "Let's go out into the fields." And while they were in the field, Cain attacked his brother, Abel, and killed him.

Afterward the Lord asked Cain, "Where is your brother? Where is Abel?"

"I don't know," Cain responded. "Am I my brother's guardian?"

But the Lord said, "What have you done? Listen! Your brother's blood cries out to me from the ground! Now you are cursed and banished from the ground, which has swallowed your brother's blood. No longer will the ground yield good crops for you, no matter how hard you work! From now on you will be a homeless wanderer on the earth."

Cain replied to the Lord, "My punishment is too great for me to bear! You have banished me from the land and from your presence; you have made me a homeless wanderer. Anyone who finds me will kill me!"

The LORD replied, "No, for I will give a sevenfold punishment to anyone who kills you." Then the LORD put a mark on Cain to warn anyone who might try to kill him. So Cain left the LORD's presence and settled in the land of Nod, east of Eden.

(Genesis 4:1-16)

To summarize, Cain and Abel both brought offerings to God. Cain's wasn't found acceptable while Abel's was. Cain's response was to get angry and even homicidal. In one moment of rage, he killed his own brother and ruined his own life.

In this story, Cain faces a difficult circumstance; his offering is not accepted by God. While there are many theologians that theorize why Cain's gift wasn't accepted, Scripture doesn't tell us explicitly. So, we actually don't know the *why*. Sometimes that summarizes life. We can guess at why certain things happen, but sometimes we won't understand what God is doing. There is something, however, that we can always control: our response.

Cain's future was marked because of his choice to murder his brother. We might find ourselves in situations all the time that we don't understand. We might say, "Why God?" every single day. And every day, we have a choice between life or death. Cain could have responded differently—after all, God told him that "you will be accepted if you do what is right." But Cain didn't listen—and was exiled from Eden.

A FATHER EXPOSED

Noah is marked in history as a great man and a great father. Even if you've never been to church, you probably know the story of this incredible guy. His obedience, faith and integrity got God's attention. His trust in God in spite of the mocking he probably faced for building an ark for a flood that was yet to come can encourage us to stay on course and watch God's plan prevail.

Noah's sons Ham, Japheth, and Shem got front rows seats to watching their dad radically obey God. In Genesis 6 and 7, we see that Noah built an ark with his hands (before the days of power tools), gathered every animal on earth (two of every kind), and faithfully waited for the rain to come. When the rains came, Noah led his family and ultimately saw the fulfilment of the promise God gave him.

This father set an example to his sons of righteousness and faithfulness.

But guess what! Noah wasn't perfect- and neither is your spiritual father! In Genesis 9, we see that the man who had just saved humanity in an act of obedience to God was now drunk, naked, and passed out. More importantly, we see how his sons chose to respond.

> *The sons of Noah who came out of the boat with their father were Shem, Ham, and Japheth. (Ham is the father of Canaan.) From these three sons of Noah came all the people who now populate the earth.*
>
> *After the flood, Noah began to cultivate the ground, and he planted a vineyard. One day he drank some wine he had made, and he became drunk and lay naked inside his tent. Ham, the father of Canaan, saw that his father was naked and went outside and told his brothers. Then Shem and Japheth took a robe, held it over their shoulders, and backed into the tent to cover their father. As they did this, they looked the other way so they would not see him naked.*
>
> *When Noah woke up from his stupor, he learned what Ham, his youngest son, had done. Then he cursed Canaan, the son of Ham:*
>
> *"May Canaan be cursed! May he be the lowest of servants to his relatives."*
>
> *Then Noah said, "May the Lord, the God of Shem, be blessed, and may Canaan be his servant! May God expand the territory of Japheth! May Japheth share the prosperity of Shem and may Canaan be his servant."*
>
> *Noah lived another 350 years after the great flood. He lived 950 years, and then he died.*
>
> (Genesis 9:18-29)

All of the sons of Noah had a choice here: to expose their father's faults, or to cover their father's faults. Ham exposed his father's faults; he "chose his own adventure" and brought a curse on himself, while Shem and Japheth covered their father and brought blessing on themselves.

As spiritual sons, we will get to see some of the most amazing triumphs and miracles in the lives of our spiritual fathers. We will see integrity and faith like no other. But we will also see humanity in all its weakness. How will we respond when we see our spiritual fathers' faults? What choice will we make? We can either bring focus on our spiritual fathers' flaws, or honor them by covering their faults and highlighting their strengths.

Remember, Noah was the only man on the planet that "found favor in the eyes of the Lord" (Genesis 6:8 NIV)—and he still had his moments! Your spiritual father might also be a great man, but he will also have weaknesses and flaws. It depends on *our* choices to forgive them their faults and cover them. Ultimately, the right decision will result in the right story ending.

ALL FOR A BOWL OF STEW

In the case of Jacob and Esau, we see two brothers with the same family upbringing, but Esau had a greater right to inheritance as a firstborn. Here's an example of a man with positive circumstances, and he *still* made the wrong choice. Cain faced a difficult or unexpected outcome; the sons of Noah had to deal with their father's own shortcomings. Esau, on the other hand, had it all going for him. But he threw it away because of a bad decision.

> *As the boys grew up, Esau became a skillful hunter. He was an outdoorsman, but Jacob had a quiet temperament, preferring to stay at home. Isaac loved Esau because he enjoyed eating the wild game Esau brought home, but Rebekah loved Jacob.*
>
> *One day when Jacob was cookiing some stew, Esau arrived home from the wilderness exhausted and hungry. Esau said to Jacob, "I'm starved! Give me some of that red stew!" (This is how Esau got his other name, Edom, which means "red.")*
>
> *"All right," Jacob replied, "but trade me your rights as the firstborn son."*
>
> *"Look, I'm dying of starvation!" said Esau. "What good is my birthright to me now?"*

But Jacob said, "First you must swear that your birthright is mine." So Esau swore an oath, thereby selling all his rights as the firstborn to his brother, Jacob.

Then Jacob gave Esau some bread and lentil stew. Esau ate the meal, then got up and left. He showed contempt for his rights as the firstborn.

(Genesis 25:27-34)

The rights of a firstborn would have included "head of household" status, plus his father's entire estate. In a moment of fleshly weakness, Esau passed all of this up for a bowl of lentil soup. Not even a tasty roast or piece of steak. We're talking soup.

What we can learn from this story of Esau and Jacob goes deeper than shock at this guy's incredible appetite for lentils.

Esau passed up an inheritance that would have transformed his future and brought him wealth and honor in exchange for immediate gratification. He responded to his rumbling stomach, instead of keeping his future in mind. And he suffered the consequences.

When things are going pretty well for us, we still need to make the right decisions in order to honor and to steward the blessings God has given us. We might have a promising future in ministry, a pricey education lined up for us, or a wonderful family. In those cases, we still choose to walk in destiny and purpose, in the choices we make daily. Esau "showed contempt for his rights" and he lost his blessings and his great circumstances.

In all of these stories, we see sons who did not determine their own circumstances. Cain's offering wasn't found acceptable; Ham, Japheth, and Shem were faced with a father who was acting out; and Esau had the rights of a firstborn lined up for him. What they did have control over were their decisions—ultimately decisions that would affect their destinies.

I guarantee that regardless of where you find yourself now, you have decisions and choices in front of you that will affect your identity and destiny as a son.

Here are a few quick principles to help guide us to make good decisions every day, in every circumstance.

LIFE HACKS FOR WISE DECISION-MAKING (FOR SPIRITUAL SONS)

1. Don't make decisions based on where you're at, but where you're going. If you would like to eventually pastor a 1,000 person-church, but your church only has 25 members, keep your end vision as the goal. Act like who God has called you to be, not who you perceive yourself to be now.

2. Be Spirit-led not flesh-led. Lentil soup? Enough said.

3. Don't settle for what you've seen as the only choice for destiny. Never settle for a dinky aquarium when an ocean of promises is available to you. Think big.

4. Hang out with people who are emotionally healthy. It's hard to make wise decisions if you and the people you hang around are addicted to dysfunction.

5. Ask yourself to "play the tape forward." *What will happen in the future if I do this?* I'm pretty sure if Cain had asked himself this key question, we might see a very different outcome in this family drama.

6. When you make a good choice, celebrate! It will build your faith for more good choices in the future.

7. Never make a decision based on emotional hurt. Make decisions that will have a healthy outcome, even if it hurts your pride (again, think of Cain feeling envious and even rejected).

8. Learn from the failures of others. You don't have to fail first before making a good decision.

9. Choose the Kingdom of God over ambition or opportunity for position. It may seem to delay your advancement, but this will always position you for a higher calling.

10. When the going gets tough, don't get going. Make a choice to stand, rather than flee during difficult circumstances and you'll reap the rewards.

LIFE HACKS FOR WISE COUNSEL
(FOR SPIRITUAL FATHERS)

1. If we try to force integrity on spiritual sons they may run. Teach your sons how to hear from God and they will *choose* integrity, knowing it's from the Lord.

2. Don't cut off spiritual sons who have made poor choices. The father of the Prodigal Son waited and hoped for his return. Would your spiritual sons feel comfortable enough to return to you after screwing up?

3. Talk dreams and vision with your spiritual sons. What do you see in their futures? How can they get there? Sometimes sons settle for less than they were made for because they didn't know any better.

4. If you want to encourage spiritual sons from your own life, rehash the times you made decisions that were tough but that had good fruit.

5. Many of us have had unhealthy relationships with our biological fathers. Spiritual sons need grace, discipline, and love demonstrated in order to learn and step into sonship.

CHAPTER FOUR

WHAT'S YOUR DNA?

Do you know that you carry identity and authority that has been given to you freely as a spiritual son?

I call this your *spiritual DNA*—and how you choose to steward this key part of your identity will affect the outcome of your destiny.

Growing up, I used to tell anyone who would listen, "My dad could beat up your dad."

Like I talked about in Chapter One, my adoptive father was a man named Victor Campbell, who became as close to me as any biological father ever could be. When he died in a tragic boating accident the day before his 50th birthday, he was pastoring a thriving church in the north of Seattle. But Victor hadn't always been a pastor.

In fact, before he was a Christian he was a motorcycle racer and had even been known to start brawls. Victor was strong and definitely scrappy, but I still exaggerated his strengths and fighting skills so that he could beat up anyone- even Chuck Norris! In my eyes, my dad was unbeatable, a fortress of brute strength and muscle.

Unlike most of us, the sons of King David didn't have to exaggerate the physical capabilities or the reputation of their natural father. We learn in the Old Testament that King David was like a modern-day superhero. Think Jackie Chan, Superman, and Elvis all rolled into one incredible dude. He was the man that stepped up to the plate to defeat the nine-foot tall Goliath, a giant that was feared by all of

Israel. He killed a lion and a bear with his own bare hands and won great military exploits. David left a legacy that has lasted thousands of years, lived a life of bravery and purpose, and was included in the lineage of Jesus.

And yet all of his 20 sons fell short of their own destinies. Amnon self-destructed by committing a terrible crime. Absalom was devoured by bitterness and revenge. Others, like Chileab, didn't self-annihilate—but they didn't exactly leave glorious legacies either. And the list goes on.

All of the sons of David were called to greatness and set up to accomplish incredible feats for the Kingdom of God. Just look at their father! So, what stopped them from achieving the potential that was hiding in their DNA?

I believe it was because they didn't understand that they already had access to the DNA of a warrior, King, military strategist, and radical worshipper of God. Each of David's sons had an opportunity to make a difference. And yet we read that most of them wrecked their own lives. A few committed brutal crimes like rape and homicide. Some of them tried to exalt themselves above their own father in a spirit of self-promotion. Others didn't do much at all. They never left their mark on anything, much less the history of the Kingdom of God.

The sons of David hadn't caught hold of what their father had earned, fought for, and learned, and they suffered the consequences.

The spiritual DNA that has been passed on to me has set me up for success and has helped me overcome weakness. But it didn't come without fighting – literally.

THE DNA OF A FIGHTER

When I was kid, all I wanted for my 12th birthday was a puppy. I'll never forget the day that my parents presented me with that perfect gift, a black lab we named Wally. It was my responsibility to take Wally on walks, so soon after my birthday, my friend Aaron and I took him around the neighborhood in Lynnwood, Washington where I grew up. Being a puppy, Wally was just happy to be on his leash, bounding around and exploring this great new world. But as we passed by Steven Hill's house, Wally's world- and mine- changed pretty quickly.

Steven Hill was one of those kids who had a full beard since he was eight years old. He was big and burly, definitely not someone you'd want to mess with on the playground. As Wally, Aaron, and I passed by Steven's house, he and his crew of other overgrown sixth graders were hanging out in the front yard. Looking to start a fight, they started making fun of Wally. They called us names, threw rocks, and even ended up kicking my puppy. I was totally overwhelmed. I felt completely helpless, powerless to stand up against Steven Hill and his motley crew to defend my innocent pet.

So, I ran. I ran all the way home, crying hysterically with Aaron and Wally trying to keep up behind me.

When I got home, my father could see I was upset and immediately asked me what was wrong. By this point, I was crying so hard you could barely makes sense of what I was saying between big gasps and snot running down my face. Eventually I told him about Steven and his gang and how they kicked Wally. What my father said next both shocked me and changed my life at the same time.

"Son, wipe away your tears, and go finish walking Wally. I want you to walk right by this Steven's house—again. And if he tries what he did before—if he starts making fun of you or Wally, or if he looks like he's gonna try to kick him again, I want you to go psycho on him. Punch him, swing your fists, kick him until you beat the snot out of this kid. Wail on him until you can't hit him anymore."

Did I mention my father was a pastor? Did I mention our current sermon series was about the peace of God? Did my father- and my pastor- just say to turn the other cheek? Or did he say to *hit* the other cheek?

When my dad gave me this advice, I must have looked confused. He reassured me again: "Wail on him." I did as he said. I wiped away my tears and put Wally back on his leash to go finish our walk. We left the house and sure enough, Steven and his gang spotted us making our way down the sidewalk. And sure enough, he and his crew made a beeline to attack me and Wally.

I stood my ground, and as Steven came closer, I took a wild swing at him. Maybe it was the "crane" from *Karate Kid*, but something connected to the kid and he went down. I was on top of the world. I had defeated my enemy, the nine-foot Goliath with brute force and raw aggression. I had won!

You can imagine my surprise at hearing my dad's voice behind me at that moment. He had actually followed behind in his car to watch me, to guide me through my battle. The moment Steven went down, he was there to keep me in the ring. He didn't quote a scripture or give me a pastoral one-liner. Instead, he said again,

"Wail on him."

I thought, *but he's already down*. But my pastor had said it again- wail on him. So I did, for what seemed like an eternity (probably about 15 seconds). Finally, my dad told me to stop swinging and to tell Steven and his gang one thing:

"Never hit me or my dog again."

Now that Steven had experienced my wrath, that single statement carried a lot of authority. In that moment, my dad taught me something. He wasn't condoning violence or training me to be the next Mike Tyson. He was teaching me a key life lesson, a nugget of truth that has been ingrained into my DNA: don't ever allow yourself to be bullied.

Fast forward almost 25 years, when my wife Rachel and I came into leadership positions at a primarily white church in rural North Carolina.

Rachel and I had a heart to grow a diverse congregation and leadership team with people of every color. Unfortunately, there were many well-meaning people that were steeped in tradition who were not happy with us, the young couple trying to introduce more diversity in the church. We had many "Stevens" at that church who disagreed with our vision, and thought they could bully us in to quitting or running away.

But because of what my father had taught me that afternoon in my childhood neighborhood, I had the fortitude and strength to stand. Instead of backing down, I actually "wailed" on the racism. I refused to change our leadership choices, and even paid for billboards on the highways that said "Laundry is the only thing that should be separated by color." Ultimately, we became one of the most racially diverse and welcoming churches in the area.

But we had to fight to get there.

Standing up against aggression and injustice had become a part of my spiritual DNA. My father had taught me to fight for my future by standing my ground and being confident in my authority—and he had taught me to keep fighting until I was sure that my enemy was destroyed.

THE DNA OF A KING

The spiritual DNA of my father included the willingness and the determination to fight. Like I said, my father had been a scrappy guy, a brawler before he became a Christian. Although this definitely looked different after he began to follow Jesus, he still knew how to stand up for himself, for truth, and for justice. He ingrained that into me because he had learned it himself.

Can you imagine what was contained in the spiritual DNA of King David?

David was one of the greatest warriors in the history of Israel. When he killed Goliath as just as a kid with a slingshot and a rock he basically established himself as the greatest underdog of all time. Later in life, he would make incredible military exploits as a brilliant military strategist. When Saul asked for 100 foreskins, David returned with 200 (1 Samuel 18:27). David won everywhere he went (2 Samuel 8:14). He defeated the Ammonites from behind (2 Samuel 10). He never did the same thing that he had done before. His war-time strategies and methods are still studied today for their efficiency and inventiveness.

Not only was David a military genius and mighty warrior, he was a great spiritual leader and passionate worshipper of God. He wrote 73 of the 150 Psalms in the Hebrew Bible, showing us what it looks like to worship God in all circumstances, to trust in His goodness and His faithfulness, *and* to be raw and real with Him. David danced before the Ark of the Covenant "with all his might" (2 Samuel 6:14 NIV), displaying to all of Israel just how much he loved the One who had led him into victory in battle. And lastly, David is called a man after God's own heart (1 Samuel 13:14 KJV). As a believer in God, that's pretty much the greatest endorsement you can get—better than a million followers on Instagram or your own reality TV show.

David's sons missed out. They had the DNA of a giant-killer, yet killed no giants. They had the greatest songwriter as a father, yet wrote no songs. They had a father who annihilated thousands of Philistines, yet never took down a single one themselves. Their spiritual father had organized the entire army *and* developed a system for all priestly duties, even singing. And yet none of his sons developed systems and orders with the same long-lasting legacy.

The wisdom, strength, and passion that was David's was also available to every one of his 20 sons. Yet, we only see one of his sons-Solomon- that even came close to demonstrating the same heart as his father.

THE DNA OF A SON

DNA is passed on from parent to child, father to son. It's the framework that makes up who someone is on a fundamental level, and it's mostly unchangeable. You can't alter your DNA by changing your circumstances or even your perspective. It's stronger than a personality attribute and more powerful than a physical condition. It's *who you are*.

The most amazing thing about DNA is that it replicates itself. That is, you don't have to strive or to struggle to get into your system. If you're a part of a family or a lineage, the DNA of that family will recreate itself in you.

Spiritual DNA may not be passed on biologically, but just as my father ingrained the DNA of a fighter into me through giving me instruction and guiding me, spiritual fathers have DNA that they can and want to pass on to their spiritual sons through relationship and mentorship.

The thriving ministries of our spiritual fathers didn't just land in their laps. They have fought battles, earned scars, and even experienced defeats that have gotten them to where they are. As spiritual sons, we can build on the foundations that they have established with their blood, sweat, and tears. However, some of us have become spectators of the calling of our leaders and mentors. Instead of knowing that we ourselves have been promised the same DNA and legacy of those who have gone before us, we sit on the sidelines to applaud their accomplishments.

The reality is that we have been called to take the same territory and go beyond even where they have, to accomplish new dreams. We are meant to grow, not regress. Not only that, we are meant to *multiply* what they have done for the Kingdom of God. As we step out in faith on the foundations of our spiritual fathers, we will see their dreams and accomplishments being expanded beyond what we could ever imagine.

When I moved to Los Angeles with my family and a few others to plant a church, I didn't have a church building waiting for me. And in a city like Los Angeles, where rent and property are incredibly expensive, it took more faith for me to believe that we would have our own place than in say, the Bible belt. But I came with the knowledge that my own spiritual father had been given buildings and facilities for the churches he had planted himself. I was confident that this blessing was a part of my DNA. I believed that because he had "gained territory" through church-planting that I would also gain territory, even in LA.

I was right. Within six months our church plant went from setting up and tearing down Sunday service in the basement of a Presbyterian church to being given nearly full use of a facility in an incredible location in one of the most expensive areas in the country.

Why were we given a church building so quickly?

I believe it was because it is in the DNA of my spiritual father to receive and establish houses of God for people to gather, learn, and worship. As a result of his legacy, we have been able to take new ground in the city of Los Angeles (literally), and build a thriving church plant where people can gather any day of the week to fellowship, encourage one another, and worship.

As the spiritual sons of great leaders, pioneers, and groundbreakers in the Kingdom of God, we can't miss out on the legacy of our fathers. There are too many people who don't know Jesus yet, who need us to step into our callings and purpose so that we can advance love, hope, and salvation in this world. Not only that, but our spiritual fathers have built up skills in the natural. They are entrepreneurs, gifted communicators, and masters of systems and procedures. By building on their skill sets and spiritual foundations, we don't have to think in terms of reaching hundreds of people. We can begin to dream about reaching millions!

Because we have the spiritual DNA of our spiritual fathers, we should be going above and beyond their own incredible accomplishments. We should know and teach God's Word on a deeper level, author more books that teach about Him, write more songs that glorify Him, and reach more people with His truth.

It is your right and your calling to walk in your spiritual father's pedigree. When we receive spiritual DNA by faith, we can step into purpose and calling above what we ever dreamed of.

This book is about becoming better spiritual sons. And one way that we become better sons is to learn, replicate, and multiply what our spiritual fathers have done. Whoever or whatever your "Steven" is, your spiritual father can help give you the tools to wail on him!

As spiritual sons and spiritual fathers, we are responsible to discover, define, carry, and impart spiritual DNA.

Here are some questions that will help you on the journey:

FOR SPIRITUAL SONS:

1. What are the three greatest character traits that you identify in your spiritual father?

2. What are the three greatest accomplishments of your spiritual father?

3. Of those traits and accomplishments, what do you feel God is calling you to possess and replicate?

FOR SPIRITUAL FATHERS:

1. What are the three greatest character traits that you identify in yourself?

2. What are the three greatest accomplishments that you have personally achieved?

3. Who have you identified as someone that can grab hold of the foundation you have laid?

CHAPTER FIVE

CRUCIAL CONVERSATIONS

I'll never forgot the time I was ministering in Denver, Colorado, at the church of a pastor who was also a spiritual father to me. I was sitting in the front row before going up to preach when he grabbed my knee, squeezed it hard, and told me, "Israel, never use the pulpit to be crass or to get a cheap laugh."

"Anyone can be funny or crude, but if you want to reach influential people, preach the Word," he continued.

He then stopped squeezing my leg. My knee still twitches to this day whenever I stray off in my preaching.

In that short moment of communication, my spiritual father warned me of a trap that he had seen many fall into. He reached out to me as a son, giving me guidance gleaned from years of preaching with spiritual generals like Oral Roberts. His advice changed my life as a pastor and preacher forever.

If we can receive from the men who mentor us, we will find ourselves further down the trek of our destiny with a stronger foundation.

But it's not always easy to communicate with the men who have major influence in our lives. We might find it hard to initiate with them or to be open about asking for advice or help. We might think it's easier to just go to a close friend or peer. Or, we might want to avoid those conversations altogether, believing we can "make it" without anyone else's input.

Doesn't always work out, does it?

REPEATING THE MISTAKES OF HIS FATHER

Amnon was the firstborn son of David. Can you imagine being King David's son? I'm sure that was a lot of pressure, but I bet it came with some great perks. Scripture tells us he had a huge house, innumerable servants, and he was heir apparent to the throne. Amnon could have made it big if he had learned from his own father's mistakes.

However, what we see in Scripture is a man who repeated a generational sin (lust), by committing a terrible and gruesome crime in raping his own sister. Amnon's actions could have been avoided. Instead, they had profound consequences, wounding many and eventually leading to his own murder.

> *Now David's son Absalom had a beautiful sister named Tamar. And Amnon, her half brother, fell desperately in love with her. Amnon became so obsessed with Tamar that he became ill. She was a virgin, and Amnon thought he could never have her.*
>
> *But Amnon had a very crafty friend—his cousin Jonadab. He was the son of David's brother Shimea. One day Jonadab said to Amnon, "What's the trouble? Why should the son of a King look so dejected morning after morning?"*
>
> *So Amnon told him, "I am in love with Tamar, my brother Absalom's sister."*
>
> *"Well," Jonadab said, "I'll tell you what to do. Go back to bed and pretend you are ill. When your father comes to see you, ask him to let Tamar come and prepare some food for you. Tell him you'll feel better if she prepares it as you watch and feeds you with her own hands."*
>
> *So Amnon lay down and pretended to be sick. And when the King came to see him, Amnon asked him, "Please let my sister Tamar come and cook my favorite dish as I watch. Then I can*

eat it from her own hands." So David agreed and sent Tamar to Amnon's house to prepare some food for him.

When Tamar arrived at Amnon's house, she went to the place where he was lying down so he could watch her mix some dough. Then she baked his favorite dish for him. But when she set the serving tray before him, he refused to eat. "Everyone get out of here," Amnon told his servants. So they all left.

Then he said to Tamar, "Now bring the food into my bedroom and feed it to me here." So Tamar took his favorite dish to him. But as she was feeding him, he grabbed her and demanded, "Come to bed with me, my darling sister."

"No, my brother!" she cried. "Don't be foolish! Don't do this to me! Such wicked things aren't done in Israel. Where could I go in my shame? And you would be called one of the greatest fools in Israel. Please, just speak to the King about it, and he will let you marry me."

But Amnon wouldn't listen to her, and since he was stronger than she was, he raped her. Then suddenly Amnon's love turned to hate, and he hated her even more than he had loved her. "Get out of here!" he snarled at her.

"No, no!" Tamar cried. "Sending me away now is worse than what you've already done to me."

But Amnon wouldn't listen to her. He shouted for his servant and demanded, "Throw this woman out, and lock the door behind her!"

So the servant put her out and locked the door behind her. She was wearing a long, beautiful robe, as was the custom in those days for the King's virgin daughters. But now Tamar tore her robe and put ashes on her head. And then, with her face in her hands, she went away crying.

Her brother Absalom saw her and asked, "Is it true that Amnon has been with you? Well, my sister, keep quiet for now, since he's your brother. Don't you worry about it." So Tamar lived as a desolate woman in her brother Absalom's house.

When King David heard what had happened, he was very angry. And though Absalom never spoke to Amnon about this, he hated Amnon deeply because of what he had done to his sister.

(2 Samuel 13:1-22)

After reading this story, most people might initially make two conclusions: a) Amnon had a major lust problem, and b) he obviously lacked self-control. And while both those things were probably true of him, I wonder if there was a deeper issue at the root of these sins: Amnon had never had what I call a *crucial conversation* with his father David.

Let me explain:

The Bible says that Amnon loved (lusted after) Tamar, his sister. Isn't it interesting that if there was one person on the planet that could have helped, understood, encouraged, and prayed for Amnon, it would have been David? Amnon's father had also lusted after a woman that was beautiful and forbidden: Bathsheba. When David committed adultery with her, he experienced the ugly effects of sin on himself, his friends, his family, and his army (see 2 Samuel 11 for the full story).

Amnon was clearly struggling with this sin. The text says that he was *so obsessed that he became ill* (2 Samuel 13:2). Amnon could have approached his father David for help with this temptation.

Instead, Amnon talked to his creepy friend Jonadab about his problem. And we all know how that ended. Jonadab formulated a plot to help Amnon succeed in succumbing to sin and ruining his own life and the life of his sister.

Even while Tamar was fighting off being raped, she begged Amnon to talk to David. But he refused. Instead he brought her incredible shame and dishonor, and basically ruined her chances at ever getting married or having her own family.

COMMUNICATION IS KEY

Let's go back further in the story. Why didn't Amnon go to David for help with his struggle? The crucial conversation could have gone something like this:

A: *Hey dad, I think I'm in love with Tamar. I don't know what to do about it, but I do have one idea...*

D: *Bad idea son! Here's why...*

I'm confident that David would have instructed him not to succumb to his lust. His own experience with Bathsheba would have given him a perspective that can only be earned from someone who has *gone through the battle himself,* and experienced the ugly consequences. David could have helped prevent Amnon from destroying his sister's life and his own life. And ultimately, his advice would have also brought greater redemption to his own sordid past.

But from our limited perspective, the conversation never happened.

So, why didn't Amnon approach his father for advice? We can't be 100% sure of the answer, but I've got a couple of theories that might help us understand why key communication between fathers and sons sometimes doesn't happen.

Dad is difficult to communicate with.

Scripture indicates that David wasn't always very approachable. Throughout the Old Testament, we see how difficult it could be for people to have important conversations with him. Although he was most likely a great speaker in front of crowds, the King of Israel may not have been easy to reach in a one-on-one conversation.

The prophet Nathan and the commander of the Israelite army Joab both resorted to some pretty ingenious ways to get the attention of David, and to help him open up.

In 2 Samuel 12, we see first serious example of David needing "creative communication." After committing adultery with Bathsheba and then plotting the death of her husband on the battlefield, David was obviously in need of some serious guidance—and for someone to give him the straight truth.

Being a prophet and a spiritual advisor to the King, Nathan went to David to confront him about what he'd done. But in order to get his point across to the King, he had to tell him a story about a rich man who unjustly took the poor man's only lamb to feed another, selfishly depriving him for his own gain. David was righteously angry in response, and Nathan revealed that *he* was the rich man of the story, as he had taken the army commander's only wife for himself. David was deeply convicted, but Nathan had to be creative to initially get the point across to him.

And then, in 2 Samuel 14:1-20, David's commander-in-chief, Joab, orchestrated an elaborate scheme to confront David about his relationship with his son Absalom, whom he had banished for avenging the rape of his sister. Joab directed a woman to dress up as a widow and come to David for wisdom about a fabricated story in which one of her sons had killed the other. Through processing this situation, David understood the truth: he needed to rectify his relationship with his own son Absalom.

David may have been difficult to reach out to, but it was possible to effectively communicate with him. Recognizing that these conversations needed to take place, both Nathan and Joab got crafty in their approach, knowing what would catch the attention of the King.

There is wisdom in understanding how our spiritual fathers receive information, and what makes them "tick" or respond. I once instructed a spiritual son to use a football analogy as a means to have a tricky conversation with his biological father, who didn't necessarily respond to emotional cues. This young man tried it, and it was effective. Whatever you do, don't let an important topic go unaddressed because it seems too difficult to address. Be creative!

Dad is intimidating.

Even though David was his biological father, Amnon was probably intimidated by this man who had killed Goliath at age 14, remodeled the tabernacle of God, and boldly danced before the ark in his underwear. Not to mention, he played the harp and could drop some serious lyrics on you.

Most spiritual fathers are intimidating. Often, they are legends of faith, leaders who we admire and look up to *because* of their experience earned from gaining victories in battle after battle.

It's this very reason that we need wisdom of our spiritual fathers. They know how to overcome trials and how to advance in their callings. It's not always easy to begin crucial conversations, especially with men who we look up to, but it's always worth it.

I once had lunch with Bishop TD Jakes and just a couple other people (I'm not trying to name drop…In fact I was just talking to Oprah about how I hate that). In my opinion, TD Jakes is one of the greatest preachers, leaders and entrepreneurs of this generation. So of course, I was intimidated by the guy! But I didn't want to let an opportunity to learn from him escape me.

During this time, I was making a decision about whether or not to move my entire family from North Carolina to Los Angeles. We would be starting from scratch to plant a brand-new church in an unfamiliar place. I was in such great need of wisdom and insight, I overcame the "intimidation factor" and asked the Bishop about his own move from West Virginia to Dallas.

He responded by giving me insight into how to make a difficult transition and rely on God in every circumstance. His wisdom and his encouragement helped my wife and me take the leap, and not long after we left our comfort zone in North Carolina to move to LA.

It wasn't easy to put myself out there and approach this spiritual father for wisdom. But he was ready and willing to respond, and more than capable of teaching me what I needed to know. Spiritual fathers want their sons to go beyond their own achievements and successes. But sometimes they are too busy to know you need their help and advice…you have to raise your hand and say, "I need your wisdom!"

Don't phone a friend.

Amnon did receive council from someone, but not from his father, which cost him his life. Spiritual fathers will tell you what you *should* hear, not necessarily what you *want* to hear.

Years ago, I became so frustrated in a ministry position that I told one of my spiritual fathers that I was going to go maverick, quit, and move to California. He pointed out some of the flaws in my perspective, warning me that I wasn't ready yet to strike out on my own. I needed a stronger foundation before launching into this part of my calling. Ultimately, I did end up in California 13 years later, as a healthier, wiser man under the covering of a spiritual father.

Amnon received his council from his friend Jonadab, described as crafty but not necessarily wise. "Make it work," was his approach. Amnon was looking for someone who would tell him what he wanted to hear. It's easy to find people we know that will take our side, or even give us good advice but not God Advice. It's funny how instead of going up for advice from his father, or even going to his own peers (his brothers), Amnon went down to someone who wasn't even in the royal lineage of David. He went to someone easy and familiar instead of someone who may have been more intimidating, but could have warned him, helped him, and encouraged him to be wise.

Pride comes before the....

Amnon may have been too prideful to ask for help from David, not wanting to reveal his lust for his sister to this man whom he admired and looked up to as a man of God. Instead, he found it easier to keep this temptation hidden from his father, which ultimately magnified the sin instead of breaking it off.

Often, we don't ask for help from our spiritual fathers because we are too embarrassed to let them see our flaws. This is a major form of pride. As a pastor, I've seen individuals with serious addictions not admit their problems to others until it's too late. Wanting to hide their shame from others, they avoid deeper relationships in their church communities or with their spiritual mentors. When their addictions are finally exposed, the damage has been done, both to themselves and to the lives of those closest to them.

Especially in our relationships to those we look up to, we may want to present who we *aspire* to be, and not who we actually are. The reality is, however, that there aren't many situations we are currently dealing with that our fathers haven't already faced. Some of our mentors have had victory, and some have had failures. Either way, they now have the wisdom to help us through challenges of every kind. David had a wealth of knowledge from his own experience with adultery, but was never asked to give his insight. By the time he was involved, it was too late for Amnon. The deed was done and destruction ensued.

HAVING "THE TALK"

The story we've learned from today is an ugly one, in which lives were destroyed by sin. Amnon could have become King of Israel and lived a long and influential life, but was ultimately killed by his brother Absalom in revenge for his sister (which we'll learn more about in Chapter Six). Tamar could have had her own children, but was forced to live in disgrace. Not to mention there must have been countless other consequences that may not be mentioned in Scripture.

Thankfully, we learn from the story of Amnon and David. More than the fact that sin is destructive, we learn that we need to learn from and communicate with our spiritual fathers. I believe that one of the saddest parts of this story is that it could have been *prevented*.

Today, marriages are being torn apart, people are quitting ministries, and sons are sabotaging their destinies because of a lack of wisdom and direction. Sons aren't receiving the wisdom, support and prayer that only fathers can give because they aren't having crucial conversations.

Having a crucial conversation relies on sons *and* fathers choosing to communicate about important decisions and tricky situations.

Here are some "life hacks" to make it easier to make those conversations happen.

HOW TO HAVE CRUCIAL CONVERSATIONS, FOR SPIRITUAL SONS

Raise your hand. People don't know what you don't tell them. Just like David, our spiritual fathers may have many sons and many responsibilities. It is difficult for them to know when you and I are struggling, unless we let them know. I promise you they want to know, and they have answers for you.

Be creative. Learn the communication language of your spiritual father. Does he prefer text? Face to face? Phone chat? Obviously King David loved stories. Nathan and Joab both used this way of communication to break the ice. What's the best way to communicate with your spiritual father? When you come to him on his own grounds, it will help him to respond effectively.

Be considerate and be clear. If your spiritual father is a pastor, never, and I mean *never* tell him "I need to talk!" before or after a church service. When you do find the opportunity to speak to him, be straightforward: "Hey Pastor Steve....I'd really like your wisdom and input on an area I'm struggling with.....when and where would be the best time and place to chat?" It's also important to communicate urgency. If it's important, say so!

Show gratitude and flexibility. When you speak to your spiritual father, don't apologize for "taking up their time." Thank them for their wisdom and their time. Spiritual leaders love to help by sharing experience and advice. If, for whatever reason, they are unable to help, ask them to recommend someone who *can* help you in the same area. For example, if it's a question about finances and they aren't sufficiently equipped to help you, ask them if they know anyone with wisdom in this area.

Be "low maintenance" and "high yield." Our spiritual fathers are often talented, gifted men with a lot to offer, so it's normal to want to spend a lot of time with them. However, consider that most of them are probably very busy with multiple obligations between ministry, work, and family. Sometimes *quality* beats *quantity* in mentoring relationships. When you do have the opportunity to meet with them, listen to their guidance. Their wisdom is valuable and should be responded to accordingly!

HOW TO HAVE CRUCIAL CONVERSATIONS, FOR SPIRITUAL FATHERS

Crucial conversations rely on both sons *and* fathers. If you are a spiritual father, here's how you can position yourself to help mentor your spiritual sons:

You're there to help. You might not know it, but you can be intimidating! Let your sons know you are there for them, to support them, encourage them, and advise them. You may think they know this...but they might not.

Communicate your availability. Let your sons know your preferred way to communicate, for example in person, phone, or email. Also, be clear about your schedule: for example, most people don't know that many pastors take Mondays off.

Be vulnerable with your sons. As your spiritual sons, we think you've always been awesome. Be open about past and even present struggles that you are overcoming. When you explain how you've gained victory, we're encouraged to know that we also have a fighting chance! It also helps us to not repeat the same mistakes.

You might need to ask us. Unfortunately, there are times that spiritual sons may feel too embarrassed to reveal what they need help with. There are times you need to *pry* it out…and if you do…you could save your spiritual sons from making some life-altering mistakes.

You don't need to have all the answers. No one expects you to be a walking Wikipedia. Offering sound advice often looks like *guiding* someone into making a wise decision, not telling them exactly what to do. Your goal as a spiritual father is not to make spiritual sons completely dependent on you, but to teach them to consistently walk in godly character.

EFFECTIVE COMMUNICATION TAKES INTENTIONALITY

Regardless of how difficult it may seem to make those crucial conversations happen, and how easy it may seem to let them slip by, I encourage both sons and fathers to not give up on this key to healthy relationship. Do whatever it takes to cross that channel of silence, and speak up! Sons, ask your spiritual fathers for advice, wisdom, and guidance. Fathers, be aware of how to be there for your sons.

These kinds of conversations can ultimately prevent destructive missteps and instill lifelong wisdom in sons. These moments are where spiritual DNA is passed on, and yes, I'm going to be dramatic—lives are changed!

CHAPTER SIX

DESTINED FOR PEACE, FALLEN TO DESTRUCTION

What do you think of when you hear the name "Absalom"?

Rebellion? Divisiveness? Violence? You may think of people who are problem starters, or who bring disunity to churches or ministries. The "Absalom Spirit" is often used to describe those who cause division or strife because of their rebellious natures.

Absalom, the third son born to King David, wasn't born to get such a bad rap. The Hebrew root word for Absalom is *shalom*, meaning "peace" or "pleasure." Some commentaries even translate his name to mean "his father's peace," and in fact, his birth did bring his father David great peace.

Absalom's birth was significant because he was the grandson of King Geshur, who ruled over a part of Syria northward from the land of Israel. As a result of this baby's lineage, the house of David was given some pretty heavy leverage during a war with Ish-Bosheth, the son of Saul who claimed that he was the rightful King of Israel. Ish-Bosheth and his army were not able to take much ground because they feared and revered King Geshur.

If Absalom was born to bring peace, then how did his identity become skewed? How did he fall into the rebellion, violence, and strife that have earned him his millennia-long reputation? Unfortunately, the story of Absalom is not a unique one. Even in the Body of Christ, we see many spiritual sons that had once been loyal "snap" and become set on destructing everything their spiritual fathers have worked so hard to establish.

The story of Absalom can help us learn *the art of sonship*, as we observe why and how this son and heir to the Kingdom of Israel acted the way he did. As we learn from his mistakes, we can step into sonship. And authentic sonship will cause us to rule and not rebel, and to become powerful through submitting to our leaders, mentors, and spiritual fathers.

CHARISMA, GOOD LOOKS, AND SOME VERY BAD DECISIONS

Absalom was a man of great charisma. He was the guy that everybody loved (2 Samuel 15:6). He is even described as the "most handsome man in all Israel" (2 Samuel 14:25). Absalom was the type of person that stood up for the people that he loved and defended those who were in trouble (2 Samuel 15:2-5). He also took care of those he loved, as it says that after his sister Tamar was raped by Amnon, he comforted her and took care of her like she was his own (2 Samuel 13:20).

Despite all of Absalom's good qualities, this charismatic, popular guy became a murderer, rebellion leader, and a rapist of 10 women. And it all started with his response to a wrong done to someone he loved.

As we read in the previous chapter, Amnon, Absalom's brother, raped his own sister Tamar in an act of violence and frankly, bad-decision making. Here, the aftermath:

> But now Tamar tore her robe and put ashes on her head. And then, with her face in her hands, she went away crying.
>
> Her brother Absalom saw her and asked, "Is it true that Amnon has been with you? Well, my sister, keep quiet for now, since he's your brother. Don't you worry about it." So Tamar lived as a desolate woman in her brother Absalom's house.

When King David heard what had happened, he was very angry. And though Absalom never spoke to Amnon about this, he hated Amnon deeply because of what he had done to his sister.

(2 Samuel 13:19-22)

This incident marked the beginning of Absalom's downward spiral into self-destruction. I believe there were four weak points about Absalom's attitude and perspective that skewed his decision-making and ultimately, his destiny.

These points can be summed up in the following facts:

- Absalom didn't like how his father handled the situation.
- He took matters into his own hands.
- He was consumed by bitterness.
- And lastly, he became prideful, eventually bringing around his own destruction.

1. COULD YOU REALLY HAVE DONE IT BETTER YOURSELF?

The Bible says that David "was very angry" (2 Samuel 13:21) when his daughter Tamar was raped, but it doesn't say that he did anything about it. Of course, it seems that the just thing to do would have been to immediately discipline his son Amnon for his crime. We hate it when people get away with doing the wrong thing, and I can only imagine how infuriated Absalom was after his father did not punish Amnon.

As a youth pastor in my twenties, I would sometimes get angry and frustrated with my senior pastor when I felt he wasn't responding correctly to people who were stubbornly stuck in their ways. To me, it was obvious that he should have just fired people who weren't fully embracing our vision and our mission. I thought he should have told critical church members, "If you don't like it you can leave."

Then, I became a senior pastor. I began to realize if you get rid of everybody you don't like, you'll be pastoring yourself at a new church called "One Church" because you'll be the only member.

David wasn't necessarily right when he neglected to punish Amnon. But if you look at the entire life of David, he was a very just and fair man. He demonstrated sound judgment, and even if he didn't deal with things right away, he dealt with them eventually. In fact, David had developed the ability to wait before immediately judging harshly. As a young man, he could even be rash. For example, when he wanted to kill Nabal immediately, but Nabal's wife talked him out of it (1 Samuel 25).

At David's death bed, he gave Solomon sound advice about how to deal with crimes that had gone unpunished:

> *As the time of King David's death approached, he gave this charge to his son Solomon:*
>
> *…"And there is something else. You know what Joab son of Zeruiah did to me when he murdered my two army commanders, Abner son of Ner and Amasa son of Jether. He pretended that it was an act of war, but it was done in a time of peace, staining his belt and sandals with innocent blood. Do with him what you think best, but don't let him grow old and go to his grave in peace.*
>
> *"Be kind to the sons of Barzillai of Gilead. Make them permanent guests at your table, for they took care of me when I fled from your brother Absalom.*
>
> *"And remember Shimei son of Gera, the man from Bahurim in Benjamin. He cursed me with a terrible curse as I was fleeing to Mahanaim. When he came down to meet me at the Jordan River, I swore by the LORD that I would not kill him. But that oath does not make him innocent. You are a wise man, and you will know how to arrange a bloody death for him."*
>
> (1 Kings 2:1, 5-9)

Clearly, David was by no means a pacifist. He didn't ignore injustice, but actually showed wisdom in timing in his response well. It wasn't always necessary to immediately react with violent retribution to a crime.

One of the greatest skills we can learn as spiritual sons is the ability to understand the "why" behind the actions of our spiritual fathers. Was there a reason why David didn't immediately punish Amnon? Was it because he was prioritizing the recent wars with the Philistines? Was it strategic because Amnon's mother had her own political ties? Was he distracted by issues with Joab, David's general, who had a temper of his own?

I'm not trying to make excuses for David's apparent lack of action. But so far in the Bible, he had been known as a just man, and a military and political strategist. We've got to guess there was a reason that he deferred punishment. But Absalom, whose name meant "peace," never tried to find out why.

He could have said:

Hey, Dad? Help me process this correctly. My sister was raped by Amnon, and you haven't done anything about it yet...can you help me understand why?

We can learn so much from our spiritual fathers if we just take the time and effort to find out the "why" behind decisions they've made that we may not understand.

I've seen too many spiritual sons become Absaloms because they became frustrated with how their spiritual fathers handled people or situations. Instead of allowing their leaders to handle conflict in their timing and wisdom, they take matters into their own hands, which brings me to my next point...

2. DON'T TAKE MATTERS INTO YOUR OWN HANDS.

It's clear that Absalom wanted retribution for this crime done to his sister. When his own father didn't respond the way he would have liked, he took matters into his own hands. He crafted a plan to kill his own brother.

Two years later, when Absalom's sheep were being sheared at Baal-hazor near Ephraim, Absalom invited all the King's sons to come to a feast. He went to the King and said, "My sheep-shearers are now at work. Would the King and his servants please come to celebrate the occasion with me?"

The King replied, "No, my son. If we all came, we would be too much of a burden on you." Absalom pressed him, but the King would not come, though he gave Absalom his blessing.

"Well, then," Absalom said, "if you can't come, how about sending my brother Amnon with us?"

"Why Amnon?" the King asked. But Absalom kept on pressing the King until he finally agreed to let all his sons attend, including Amnon. So Absalom prepared a feast fit for a King.

Absalom told his men, "Wait until Amnon gets drunk; then at my signal, kill him! Don't be afraid. I'm the one who has given the command. Take courage and do it!" So at Absalom's signal they murdered Amnon. Then the other sons of the King jumped on their mules and fled.

As they were on the way back to Jerusalem, this report reached David: "Absalom has killed all the King's sons; not one is left alive!"

(2 Samuel 13:23-30)

In a sense, Absalom "corrected" the situation and achieved what he set out to do. But in the process, he became a murderer of his own flesh and blood.

Many of us can relate to Absalom in the sense that we feel obligated to correct, or solve situations. We burden ourselves with the problems of others and end up overstepping our boundaries. The problem with Absalom was not that he took care of his sister, but that he took care of Amnon.

As children of God we must realize that when we take matters into our own hands, we tie the hands of our heavenly Father. We have to trust God and believe that His laws and principles hold true. Galatians 6:7 (ESV) says,

Do not be deceived: God is not mocked, for whatever one sows, that will he also reap.

God is just and His word is true. If someone in your life has done wrong or is doing wrong, they will "reap" their just rewards.

There have been many times in my life where I have been mistreated by pastors, leaders, friends, and even family members. In those situations, it sometimes felt like God was not doing anything about it, to defend me or to bring about justice. Satan would try to convince me to take matters into my own hands and deal with hurt by confronting my abusers or throwing them under the bus. Since God wasn't doing anything about it (or so I felt), it was my green light to take action!

When I was a youth pastor in my twenties, my senior pastor happened to *love* me…. But the Executive Pastor? Not so much. He would rebuke me openly and unnecessarily, but I refused to speak badly about him in front of those in leadership or under my leadership.

In retrospect, I believe this man was jealous because of the opportunities given to me that weren't given to him. I thank God that I did not fall into the enemy's trap. Rather than trying to bring retribution to those situations, I allowed my heavenly Father to take care of executing justice. I realized that the minute I start thinking that I can do God's job better than Him, I am in serious trouble.

3. BITTERNESS = POISON

For *two* years [Absalom] simmered, plotted, and schemed how he was going to make sure Amnon was brought to justice (2 Samuel 13:38, 14:28).

In other words, Absalom spent 730 days plotting the revenge of his sister Tamar. Anger consumed him; it took over in his life and eventually was the very thing that disqualified him from becoming King, from fulfilling his destiny.

Absalom's future was destroyed because he allowed bitterness to grow in his heart. He bided time and when opportunity came, he sought revenge. His crime was not done in the heat of the moment, but was done after two years of hatred growing deep inside him. During those two years that simmered over getting back at his brother, he did not say anything good or anything bad to Amnon (2 Samuel 13:22). And yet, resentment still grew in his heart.

If Absalom would have told his father what he was feeling, the story would have ended differently. If anyone could have related to feeling frustration at injustice, it would have been David. He could have told him about the countless times that Saul threw spears at him, ordered his assassination, even hunted after him with his army. David could have taught him how to trust God, even when he had been mistreated.

With this lesson under his belt, Absalom would have been crowned the next King of Israel. He could have been a King that built on the successes and the foundations of his own father, becoming a leader that could have surpassed him.

Instead, Absalom did what most of us do when we have been wronged. He pretended as if everything was perfectly fine, secretly plotting his revenge.

There are a lot of Christians today who have mastered the art of being fake. They have learned to put on their "church faces" and pretend that everything is peachy keen. The sad truth is, our churches may have bitter people who appear to be Christlike, but are inwardly planning on how to get back at those who have hurt them, even in the Body of Christ. They may not be thinking homicide—maybe it's angry verbal confrontation, petty insults, or "making them jealous." Whatever it may be, this kind of bitterness ultimately does the most hurt to the person who is withholding forgiveness.

The Bible urges us to "confess your trespasses to one another, and pray for one another that you may be healed" (James 5:16). When we confess our anger or unforgiveness to others, we position ourselves to receive healing. The enemy has deceived us into thinking that we should isolate ourselves and hide our pain, insecurity, and anger from the Body of Christ, creating a mindset that keeps us from our healing and our breakthrough.

Who has hurt you? Who has mistreated you? What seed of bitterness has been planted in your heart? I believe that God wants to set you free. He is asking you to turn your situation over to Him. Let us not be the sons that stand in the way of our Father, but rather be the sons that allow God to be God. Deuteronomy 32:35 (NKJV) says,

> *Vengeance is mine, and recompense; their foot shall slip in due time; For the day of their calamity is at hand, and the things to come hasten upon them.*

4. PRIDE COMES BEFORE THE FALL.

You would think that after King David gave him a clean slate, Absalom would have been the most grateful person alive. Even after committing grievous sin, he was still in line to become the King of Israel and was blessed by his father (2 Samuel 14). But instead of rising into his position rightfully, he usurped the position without integrity, and "stole the hearts of the men of Israel."

> *After this, Absalom bought a chariot and horses, and he hired fifty bodyguards to run ahead of him. He got up early every morning and went out to the gate of the city. When people brought a case to the King for judgment, Absalom would ask where in Israel they were from, and they would tell him their tribe. Then Absalom would say, "You've really got a strong case here! It's too bad the King doesn't have anyone to hear it. I wish I were the judge. Then everyone could bring their cases to me for judgment, and I would give them justice!"*
>
> *When people tried to bow before him, Absalom wouldn't let them. Instead, he took them by the hand and kissed them. Absalom did this with everyone who came to the King for judgment, and so he stole the hearts of all the people of Israel.*

(2 Samuel 15: 1-6)

Absalom used the same charisma and peace that God had given him to be a successful King for his own selfish advancement. He began to persuade the people of Israel to turn against his father, by telling them what he would do if he was anointed King of Israel.

Have you ever thought to yourself or even stated, "If I were the boss (or the pastor, or my mother, or my spouse), I would do it this way!" I know that I have made those types of remarks, until God began to deal with me and show me that those kinds of thoughts are poisonous.

When Absalom became prideful by believing he would do a better job as King than his own father, he brought about his own destruction.

In Luke 6:37-38 Jesus commands us not to judge:

Do not judge others, and you will not be judged. Do not condemn others, or it will all come back against you. Forgive others, and you will be forgiven. Give, and you will receive. Your gift will return to you in full—pressed down, shaken together to make room for more, running over, and poured into your lap. The amount you give will determine the amount you get back.

When we judge others, we condemn ourselves to the same treatment. In judging his father, Absalom himself ultimately came under great judgment for his actions. In fact, he became so notorious that his reputation lives on today. His pride ultimately resulted in his own downfall, as Proverbs 16:18 says, "Pride goes before destruction."

In a twisted spiral of judgment and pride, we see that Absalom was transformed into a violent and vengeful man. Ironically, the very crime that compelled Absalom to commit homicide was one of the first things Absalom did when he gained authority.

Then Absalom turned to Ahithophel and asked him, "What should I do next?"

Ahithophel told him, "Go and sleep with your father's concubines, for he has left them here to look after the palace. Then all Israel will know that you have insulted your father beyond hope of reconciliation, and they will throw their support to you." So they set up a tent on the palace roof where everyone could see it, and Absalom went in and had sex with his father's concubines.

(2 Samuel 16:20-22)

Absalom raped 10 of David's concubines on the roof of the palace so all of Jerusalem would see. He multiplied the crime that he first set out to correct. Instead of becoming a hero, he became more violent and evil than his own enemy.

There are so many things we can learn from the life of Absalom. It is truly a shame that his life ended with a short reign of only days (2 Samuel 15-18). He had the looks, the charisma, and the DNA of a King and a warrior, and yet he disqualified himself from his destiny by taking matters into his own hands and hiding bitterness in his heart.

Even when we screw up, rebel, or act out of pride or bitterness, we can repent. Absalom had the opportunity to receive forgiveness and redeem himself. After the murder of Amnon, he fled to his grandfather's home. His father David was left to mourn the death of his son Amnon *and* mourn the loss of his son Absalom. Just like our heavenly Father, David unconditionally desired to be with his son.

And David mourned many days for his son Amnon.

Absalom fled to his grandfather, Talmai son of Ammihud, the King of Geshur. He stayed there in Geshur for three years. And King David now reconciled to Amnon's death, longed to be reunited with his son Absalom.

(2 Samuel 13:37-39)

No matter what we have done, no matter what act we have committed in the midst of pain, God desires to restore us and to heal us. God wants to bring us to a place of security in him. Joab, seeing the cry of David's heart, called for Absalom to come back home (2 Samuel 14:1- read more about the story in Chapter Five). We read in 2 Samuel 14 that David brought Absalom in and kissed him on the head.

Then at last David summoned Absalom, who came and bowed low before the King, and the King kissed him.

(2 Samuel 14:33)

According to the law, Absalom deserved death, but David showed him grace. But Absalom didn't receive his father's grace and forgiveness.

Again, there is a great parallel to the actions of Absalom and our lives. God's grace and mercy are ever present. Yet too often we don't receive them, and continue to demolish our own destinies by stubbornly remaining in sin.

Which son will you be? Will you be the son that continues to stand in the way of your heavenly Father, or will you be the son that allows God to be God? Will you be the son that hides bitterness and pain in your heart, or will you be vulnerable and confess those things to God and to others?

God is ready to heal you, fight for you, forgive you, and give you what rightfully belongs to you, but you have to be willing to let Him.

Take a few moments and ask God to begin to reveal areas in your life in which you need healing. Ask Him to bring to your memory people that have wronged you, that you may not have forgiven. And do whatever needs to be done: call that person and reconcile your relationship, ask for forgiveness if you need to, pray for those who have hurt you. I believe that as you ask God for His perfect will to be done in your heart and relationships, you are going to experience healing, promotion, and blessing as you step into your calling and destiny.

Let's pray:

Father God, thank you that you are the God that heals me and sets me free. Holy Spirit, would you reveal to me where I am holding onto bitterness and unforgiveness, especially towards my leaders? Give me the strength and the humility to ask for their forgiveness. Help me to see them as you do. In the name of Jesus, I pray. Amen.

CHAPTER SEVEN

WHAT'S MY NAME AGAIN?

I've already shared with you my own story in Chapter One how I was born to parents addicted to drugs, abandoned as an infant, and adopted into a new family. I told the story of how my adoptive father died when I was a teenager, leaving me once again without a father.

But wait for it: the story gets even crazier. Just recently, I experienced another jacked-up twist to the plot that has made my life a testimony to redemption and God's miracle-working power. It's a crucial part of my story that has made me stand once again on my identity as a son.

Just a few years ago, my wife and I moved from North Carolina to Los Angeles to launch WaveChurch LA under the leadership of our senior pastors, Steve and Sharon Kelly. We left a lot behind to take this risk, but we were expectant, excited, and ready to see God move.

Launching a church in any city can be difficult, but Los Angeles is especially challenging. It's the entertainment capital of the world, filled with distractions, and more or less unchurched. Before we even launched our first service, we got kicked out of a building we had reserved for an entire year. We were told "no" by 42 other venues, even one sorry excuse for a facility that was basically a closet we'd have to rent for 5k a month.

Finally, we ended up in the cramped, dingy downstairs basement of a Presbyterian Church, where we met at 5 p.m. every Sunday evening. We would cram ourselves in what we called "the dungeon" to worship, pray, and learn the Word of God. It was not what we had envisioned for a booming church in LA.

During the process of looking for venues and trying to start a church, my wife's mother died in her battle with cancer. Months after that, both of her grandparents also passed. By this point, Rachel had lost her mother, her father, two of her sisters, and both her grandparents in a span of four years. She's a champion, but this was a lot to bear, especially with the stress of building a new life in a new city.

All of this added up to what I would call a rough start.

Then out of the blue, I received a Facebook message about my biological mother, the same woman who had left me on the doorstep of my aunt and uncle. Her immediate family- my family- reached out to me because they saw on Facebook that I had recently moved to Redondo Beach, California. They shared with me that my birth mom had just passed away and her body was in a mortuary in Redondo Beach.

Crazy, to say the least.

But the story doesn't end there. Her family actually asked me to perform the funeral for my deceased mother, whom I had never met.

As I prepared to speak at the service, the greatest challenge was staying grounded while trying to gather information about my mother, Diane Schwingdorf-Anders. Speaking to her sisters and brothers (my aunts and uncles) and her other son (my brother) really messed with me.

As I pieced together the events of my mom's life, I tried to place myself in it; where did I fit? Was I even important to her story? At her funeral, many of her relatives were shocked to find out that Diane had a son named Israel. I found myself feeling forgotten, like I had been kept a secret.

As I considered this bizarre coincidence, and tried to understand why she had never looked for me, I began to question my own identity, feeling lost and misplaced.

In the end, I found myself standing on my foundations as a son— both of God and of the godly men and women who had raised and discipled me. I knew that even before I was formed in my mother's womb, God had a plan and a purpose for me (Jeremiah 29:11). I discovered that because of who I am in God and what I have learned as a son, I could stand.

Every son, at one time or another, will have his identity messed with. It is one of the devil's main tactics. Even Jesus was threatened and mocked by Satan, trying to de-rail the Son of God from His destiny.

> *Then Jesus was led by the Spirit into the wilderness to be tempted there by the devil. For forty days and forty nights he fasted and became very hungry.*
>
> *During that time the devil came and said to him, "**If** you are the Son of God, tell these stones to become loaves of bread."*
>
> *But Jesus told him, "No! The Scriptures say, 'People do not live by bread alone, but by every word that comes from the mouth of God.'"*

(Matthew 4:1-4; bold added for emphasis)

If the devil tried tempting Jesus to deny Himself and to reject what He knew to be true, you better believe he's going to try the same thing with us. Which brings us to the story of Chileab.

WHO *IS* CHILEAB?

Chileab was the second son of King David, after Amnon. We don't see much of Chileab in Scripture. No great military feats or remarkable accomplishments for the Kingdom of God. This guy never seemed to be a contender to the throne, but he was still the son of David. He was given the inheritance and the right to possess the DNA of a giant killer.

The problem is, Scripture never tells us that Chileab killed any giants.

Chileab's identity seems obscured in Scripture, even to the point where he has two different names in the original text, as shown in the King James Version.

In 2 Samuel 3:3 (KJV), the second son of David is listed as "Chileab":

> And **his second, Chileab**, *of Abigail the wife of Nabal the Carmelite; and the third, Absalom the son of Maacah the daughter of Talmai King of Geshur;*

But in 1 Chronicles 3:1 (KJV), we see the second son listen as "Daniel":

> *Now these were the sons of David, which were born unto him in Hebron; the firstborn Amnon, of Ahinoam the Jezreelitess;* **the second Daniel**, *of Abigail the Carmelitess*

The same son, listed as two different people. Unfortunately, that's all we get to see of Chileab in Scripture. He's mentioned only twice, both in listings of names.

What we can assume, however, is that there were questions of Chileab being the biological son of David. King David had married his mother Abigail hastily after the death of her first husband. Many theologians theorize that she might have even been pregnant already with Chileab at that point.

Can you imagine what Chileab must have heard from people around him?

> ......*David's not really your father.*

> .....*Nabal was your father, and he's a fool! (1 Samuel 25:25)*

> ...*You don't belong.*

Whether or not the rumors could have been true, Chileab was included in the lineage of David, and a successor to the throne. His father was the King of Israel, his spiritual DNA the same of a hero and a legendary warrior. In fact, "Chileab" can even be translated to "perfection of the father."**

Legend has it that Chileab actually resembled David, although he may not have been his biological son.*** Children learn facial expressions from their parents, and how to display a physical reaction to certain events. This explains the phenomenon of a child who does not share the genetics of his parents, but who resembles his parents. That may have been the case for Chileab, who probably learned to look, walk, and talk like his dad. To reinforce the point, I look and act like my father Victor, although he wasn't my biological dad.

Whether or not Chileab was David's biological son is not the important thing; in any case, he shared the promise, the inheritance, the identity of the son of the King of Israel.

This son of David was never mentioned again in Scripture. It's possible that he never took hold of his true inheritance because he wrestled with wondering if the rumors were true...he may have thought, "I *am* a fraud and a poser. I'm not a true son."

We cannot know what Chileab was thinking or what he went through for sure, but regardless, we can learn this from his story (or lack of story): knowing your identity as a son is key to fulfilling your destiny.

IDENTITY UNDER THE FIRE

I can promise you that as a spiritual son, your identity will be questioned and tested.

Have you ever known someone in the church who was primed and prepared for leadership, a Chileab who was "second in line from the throne"—but who you never heard from again?

I wonder how many spiritual sons abdicate their spiritual inheritances because they doubt that they are true sons of the house.

Many of us become spiritual sons with baggage that causes us to feel confused about our identities. We may have histories of addiction, abuse, or mental illness, or family histories that are "complicated." We may feel like there are key pieces of our identity that are missing or unfulfilled. In my own story of recently meeting my biological family under some pretty crazy circumstances, I was forced to rethink my own lineage. Who am I, and whose am I?

Or, it may be that we come under criticism and judgement from others. We may come across people who are jealous of our callings and inheritances, and cause us to feel discouraged or unsure about what we know to be true.

One of the biggest ways we come under attack is in our own mind. We can begin to think thoughts like:

Am I even needed?

Am I even wanted?

Am I even qualified?

Am I truly a son of the house?

Do I really belong?

Is _____ really my spiritual father?

Satan will use anything to make us insecure.

One of the enemy's main tactics of derailing us from our destiny is to cause us to question what we know to be true, and to feel worn down, confused, and discouraged.

The doubt, the worry, and maybe even the whispers that say you don't belong should be destroyed by this one thing: your spiritual father (and heavenly Father) have called you "son." If you are a spiritual son, then you are in God's plan for your life.

I don't think it was by accident that David named his second son "perfection of his father." I think it was intentional. I think David knew the rumors and purposefully gave him a name that would remind his son that he belonged in his father's house.

We won't really know who Chileab's biological father was until we get to heaven and watch the whole story unfold on Blu-ray. But we do know what David proclaimed over Chileab's birth.

David said he was perfect.

STAND THE TEST

Our nation and world are facing a serious identity crisis. Everything from ethnicity issues to sexuality to abandonment issues to identity theft show that many of us are in crisis: we don't know who we are, what we're called, and how we're designed.

Above all else, we have to know our identities as sons of God. If we don't get this right first, everything else will crumble. We won't know what we're destined for. We won't know how to battle the tactics of the devil, and why we have authority.

Secondly, we have to know our identities as spiritual sons of our spiritual fathers. God designed the Kingdom to be lived out and advanced through relationships. In knowing that we come under the covering and the spiritual authority of great men of God, we will walk confidently and successfully in our destinies.

As spiritual sons, we are called:

- Leaders (Deuteronomy 28:13)
- Priests (1 Peter 2:9)
- Ambassadors (2 Corinthians 5:20)
- Heirs of the Promise (Romans 8:17)

I encourage you to declare and decree these pieces of identity over your life.

- *I was born to lead others in humility.*
- *I am called a royal priest in the house of God.*
- *I am an ambassador of Christ on earth.*
- *I am an heir to the incredible promises of God.*

When you choose to stand on your identity as a son regardless of the storms you face, the criticisms you may hear, and the questions you ask, you will find yourself well on your way to fulfilling your destiny. You won't step down from the inheritance lined up for you. And your name won't be obscured or forgotten in the lineage of the children of God.

*According to medieval theologian, Rashi. "Chileab" https://en.wikipedia.org/wiki/Chileab

** James Orange -Synoptica Hebraea: Anglo-Hebrew Bible expositor 1858 Page 32 "Chiliab, Kl-ab, perfection of, father, 2 Sam. iii."

***Ginzerb, Szold, Radin (1909) *The Legends of the Jews: From Joshua to Esther.* Baltimore, Maryland. Johns Hopkins Press.

https://www.americanadoptions.com/blog/why-do-adopted-children-look-like-their-parents/

CHAPTER EIGHT

SELF-PROMOTION KILLS DESTINY

I am not easily embarrassed by nature. It takes a *lot* for me to feel uncomfortable.

But a few years ago, I experienced a situation that made me grit my teeth and cringe—and it happened in my own church.

I have a dear friend who also happens to be a major recording artist in the Christian music industry. This woman has a Grammy, a Dove Award, and more stacked on her mantelpiece, but she's incredibly humble. One weekend, we were fortunate to have her lead worship and minister at a special worship service at our church. After her set was finished and ministry time had ended, I escorted her out on the down-low; or so I thought.

When someone in our congregation ferreted her way in our path, and immediately started belting out a worship song that this artist had recorded, I knew I hadn't been sneaky enough.

This very well-meaning (and somewhat vocally talented) person *might* have thought,

"I've been waiting to be discovered for so long. Here's my chance. If _____ hears how well I can sing *her* song, she'll definitely ask me to go on tour with her!"

Needless to say, I was mortified, and apologized profusely to my friend. But despite her Grammys, her professional experience, and the fact that she had just led a two-hour worship set, she was totally unfazed. This was routine for her. She told me that when she travels and ministers people will often "gift" her a CD they have self-produced to try and impress her. Or, if they don't have a CD, they'll just spend time *telling* her what incredible singers they are.

She went on to say, "If you're really that good, you don't *need* to promote yourself. Think of this: Rolls Royce rarely advertises but the cheapest Kia is constantly trying to advertise itself."

The point is, you don't need to prove your talent, gifts, and abilities. They will speak for themselves to people in authority or leadership, or in positions of influence.

Proverbs 18:16 says,

A man's gift makes room for him, And brings him before great men.

Unfortunately, Adonijah, the son of David, never learned that lesson.

THE GUY WE ALL AVOID

After the death of Amnon and Absalom, Adonijah was heir apparent to the throne. But instead of allowing those in authority and leadership over him (King David) to promote him in the right time and with the right intentions, Adonijah tried to promote himself into Kingship.

About that time David's son Adonijah, whose mother was Haggith, began boasting, "I will make myself King." So he provided himself with chariots and charioteers and recruited fifty men to run in front of him. Now his father, King David, had never disciplined him at any time, even by asking, "Why are you doing that?" Adonijah had been born next after Absalom, and he was very handsome.

Adonijah took Joab son of Zeruiah and Abiathar the priest into his confidence, and they agreed to help him become King. But

Zadok the priest, Benaiah son of Jehoiada, Nathan the prophet, Shimei, Rei, and David's personal bodyguard refused to support Adonijah.

Adonijah went to the Stone of Zoheleth near the spring of En-rogel, where he sacrificed sheep, cattle, and fattened calves. He invited all his brothers—the other sons of King David—and all the royal officials of Judah. But he did not invite Nathan the prophet or Benaiah or the King's bodyguard or his brother Solomon.

(1 Kings 1:5-10)

The first problem we run into with Adonijah was that he began saying "I will make myself King." He started believing his own press releases and anointed himself to be King of Israel, rather than allowing those in authority over him to raise him into leadership.

After declaring himself King, he threw a big party to celebrate his "promotion." Talk about delusional! He tried to give the illusion that he was King, without waiting to be given honor and authority by others.

Adonijah thought he had arrived by promoting himself. But what he failed to realize was that promotion only comes from God. Psalm 75:7 says:

It is God alone who judges; he decides who will rise and who will fall.

In the end, we find that Adonijah was *not* chosen to be King. His younger brother Solomon became the preferred choice after Solomon's mother, Bathsheba, and the prophet Nathan intervened.

Nathan went in and bowed before the King with his face to the ground. Nathan asked, "My lord the King, have you decided that Adonijah will be the next King and that he will sit on your throne? Today he has sacrificed many cattle, fattened calves, and sheep, and he has invited all the King's sons to attend the celebration. He also invited the commanders of the army and Abiathar the priest. They are feasting and drinking with him and shouting, 'Long live King Adonijah!' But he did not invite me or

Zadok the priest or Benaiah or your servant Solomon. Has my lord the King really done this without letting any of his officials know who should be the next King?"

King David responded, "Call Bathsheba!" So she came back in and stood before the King. And the King repeated his vow: "As surely as the LORD lives, who has rescued me from every danger, your son Solomon will be the next King and will sit on my throne this very day, just as I vowed to you before the LORD, the God of Israel."

(1 Kings 1: 23b-30)

Unfortunately for Adonijah, his plan backfired on him. By putting on a big show, he provoked Bathsheba and Nathan (both people of authority), and caused King David to reconfirm his original promise to Bathsheba to make Solomon King.

SELF-PROMOTION KILLS

The irony of self-promotion is that it actually achieves the opposite of its intended effect. Instead of fulfilling dreams and desires, it results in their death.

The spiritual son that only knows how to promote himself always gets himself killed—not because he promotes himself, but because of his *attitude* behind self-promotion.

When Solomon was crowned King of Israel, he could have easily lopped off Adonijah's head for holding a banquet during his own coronation ceremony. But instead, he had mercy on his brother, which was actually very unusual in those days of *Game of Thrones*-style Kingdom struggle.

Adonijah was afraid of Solomon, so he rushed to the sacred tent and grabbed on to the horns of the altar. Word soon reached Solomon that Adonijah had seized the horns of the altar in fear, and that he was pleading, "Let King Solomon swear today that he will not kill me!"

Solomon replied, "If he proves himself to be loyal, not a hair on his head will be touched. But if he makes trouble, he will die." So King Solomon summoned Adonijah, and they brought him down from the altar. He came and bowed respectfully before King Solomon, who dismissed him, saying, "Go on home."

(1 Kings 1: 50-53)

Notice the stipulation here: Solomon said that if Adonijah "prove[d] himself loyal," he would be in the clear. But if "he made trouble, he will die." As we see in this plot twist, Adonijah chose the wrong road, and suffered the consequences.

One day Adonijah, whose mother was Haggith, came to see Bathsheba, Solomon's mother. "Have you come with peaceful intentions?" she asked him.

"Yes," he said, "I come in peace. In fact, I have a favor to ask of you."

"What is it?" she asked.

He replied, "As you know, the Kingdom was rightfully mine; all Israel wanted me to be the next King. But the tables were turned, and the Kingdom went to my brother instead; for that is the way the LORD wanted it. So now I have just one favor to ask of you. Please don't turn me down."

"What is it?" she asked.

He replied, "Speak to King Solomon on my behalf, for I know he will do anything you request. Ask him to let me marry Abishag, the girl from Shunem."

"All right," Bathsheba replied. "I will speak to the King for you."

So Bathsheba went to King Solomon to speak on Adonijah's behalf. The King rose from his throne to meet her, and he bowed down before her. When he sat down on his throne again, the King ordered that a throne be brought for his mother, and she sat at his right hand.

"I have one small request to make of you," she said. "I hope you won't turn me down."

"What is it, my mother?" he asked. "You know I won't refuse you."

"Then let your brother Adonijah marry Abishag, the girl from Shunem," she replied.

"How can you possibly ask me to give Abishag to Adonijah?" King Solomon demanded. "You might as well ask me to give him the Kingdom! You know that he is my older brother, and that he has Abiathar the priest and Joab son of Zeruiah on his side."

Then King Solomon made a vow before the LORD*: "May God strike me and even kill me if Adonijah has not sealed his fate with this request. The* LORD *has confirmed me and placed me on the throne of my father, David; he has established my dynasty as he promised. So as surely as the* LORD *lives, Adonijah will die this very day!" So King Solomon ordered Benaiah son of Jehoiada to execute him, and* **Adonijah was put to death.**

(1 Kings 2: 13-25)

Adonijah wasn't executed for trying to become King. He was executed for showing disrespect by requesting to marry Abishag, who was King David's nurse. This request was a direct affront to the rule and authority of the King, as Abishag was also considered part of the harem of King David. In other words, she was his concubine.

Adonijah did not directly ask for the crown. Instead, he tried to undermine Solomon by being sneaky and trying to take something (or someone) that belonged to the King. At this point, he hadn't repented for his efforts at self-promotion and he hadn't given up on taking power either. In the end, his lack of self-awareness and selfishness resulted in his execution. He had his own agenda to fulfill, and not the agenda of the Kingdom.

THE ATTITUDE BEHIND SELF-PROMOTION

So many spiritual sons sabotage their futures because they won't let God promote them into positions of leadership or authority in the Church. They may want to become pastors, worship leaders, or church-planters, but they feel "stuck" in positions serving others— still the underdog. So, they take matters into their own hands and strive for position without the right opportunity, in the wrong season.

In any case, self-promotion will always destroy or prevent genuine opportunities for recognition.

In looking at the story of Adonijah, we see several root causes of why Adonijah brazenly declared himself King, and then refused to give up when he lost his chance.

Lack of discipline

The Bible says that David never disciplined Adonijah, which I believe could have been one of the reasons he tried to take things into his own hands.

If David had pulled Adonijah aside and set him straight when he began to show signs of self-promotion, he might have stopped, out of fear or repentance. But King David didn't intervene, allowing his son to behave out of turn.

As spiritual fathers, we should take note and realize we do a huge disservice to our spiritual sons when we ignore bad attitudes and unhealthy ways of thinking we observe. Sometimes we don't discipline in the form of a rebuke, but by encouraging patience, which produces self-discipline.

Hurt and rejection

When Adonijah decided he was going to declare himself King, he probably already knew that Solomon was already in line to receive the Kingship. He threw a banquet to celebrate his "Kingship", and he strategically did not invite the prophet Nathan, the King's bodyguard, or Solomon himself (1 Kings 1:10). He may have already been feeling hurt, rejected, and looked over by his family.

Arguably the greatest test to your identity as a spiritual son is when someone else gets picked over you. It's disheartening, hurtful and takes a true man of God to humbly receive and accept the situation, trust your spiritual father's decision, and ultimately, God.

One of my first positions in the Church was to help in a junior high ministry. I did *everything*: I set-up and tore-down for every weekly service, served the junior high pastor with whatever he needed, and spent long hours with a bunch of prepubescent thirteen-year old boys. Talk about sacrifice.

I gave my all to that ministry, so I'll never forget the pain, the hurt and the frustration when the junior high pastor picked someone else to be his assistant. I could have gone to our senior pastor and complained, or gone to some of the other junior high leaders and tried to convince them why I should have been picked. My motives, my response, and my behavior were tested in one of the greatest challenges of my early days in ministry.

Instead, I decided I was going to do everything I could to make the new assistant a success. I was a support to him in all that he did. By making him successful, I would become successful.

My spiritual father at the time, who was my pastor, saw my response. In a matter of months, the junior high pastor moved to another state, and I was picked as his successor.

It was God's timing—and God's way. My position as junior pigh pastor was my first staff ministry position, ultimately providing the foundation for my future as a lead pastor of multiple churches.

Oh, how I could have easily "Adonijah'd" my destiny. But I learned to trust God and my spiritual father when someone else got chosen over me, even if it hurt my pride.

DON'T "ADONIJAH" YOUR DESTINY

If Adonijah had just trusted King David's decision, I believe he could have accomplished great things for the Kingdom of God.

Hypothetically, Adonijah could have received what he desired in the first place: Kingship. Eventually, the Kingdom was given to Solomon. The Bible says that the influence of Solomon's multiple concubines caused him to slip away from God (1 Kings 11), and ultimately the Kingdom of Israel was split into two. If Adonijah had been placed in the right place at the right time, he could have received position and authority in the new Kingdom.

I'm reminded of the senior pastor of a mega church who picked a particular leader to take over for him when he stepped down. The youth pastor, who was a spiritual son of the senior pastor, could have thrown a fit for not being picked and even caused a church split over the situation. Instead, he stayed, and served the new senior pastor with respect and honor. Ultimately, he was commissioned to start a new church in a different state, which eventually became one of the most influential churches in the world.

Because this spiritual son trusted his spiritual father's decision - and trusted God - he changed the world with his ministry.

Alternatively, Adonijah could have become Solomon's right-hand man, a position that would have given him honor, respect, and power.

I've seen countless people think they were called to be senior pastors, when in reality they were more skilled at being a support to others in leadership. And I've seen some of my favorite people and ministers *know* they are called to support their leaders, and live great lives of fulfilled purpose and destiny. Often, they wield more influence in serving others than if they would have tried to do their own thing.

The Body of Christ has had many spiritual sons force their way into being Seniors Pastors, when I believe that was not what they were called to be. And just like in the case of Adonijah, they died trying to promote themselves instead of letting God do the promoting!

We don't know for certain what could have happened, but we do know that God rewards a clean heart and correct motives. Unfortunately, Adonijah had neither.

God is not mocked. Whatever we sow, we reap! (Galatians 6:7 ESV)

Will we sow division, selfishness, and self-promotion; or grace, mercy, and generosity? Coming into your destiny will sometimes require you to be humble in difficult situations and to choose to promote others.

Humble sonship in today's social media era can be difficult to navigate. We've all seen the #humblebrag hashtag. What we must realize is that most of the time when we post on Instagram, we are not posting our worst moments, but our best. I understand the importance of marketing and brand awareness, but we can't forget that promotion doesn't actually come from how many Twitter followers we have, or how many likes we get on Facebook or Instagram.

True promotion comes from God and God alone. There is so much God-given purpose on all of our lives, but we have to resist the temptation to take promotion into our own hands when it doesn't seem to be happening.

Here are four practical tools to help you maintain the correct heart attitude towards the desire for promotion.

1. REMEMBER, GOD IS IN CONTROL.

We have to know and constantly remind ourselves that God is in control. He will speak to our spiritual fathers to put us in the right place at the right time.

I know what some of you are thinking- *you don't know my Pastor!*

You are right. I don't know your Pastor, but I do know God, and He didn't leave David as a shepherd in the field, even when his own father did. God wouldn't allow David's destiny to be hidden. You can trust your heavenly Father to reward and promote you at the right time.

2. DON'T LOOK DOWN ON BEING #2.

I'd rather be a role player on a championship team like the Golden State Warriors (even though I'm a die-hard Lakers fan) than be the best player at my local YMCA. Being okay with being a support to the primary leader will ultimately give you opportunities to excel.

The senior pastor role is not necessarily the most important of the Body of Christ. Paul lets us know, there are some parts that don't get a lot of attention but without them we can't function (just think of your liver or kidneys!).

> *But our bodies have many parts, and God has put each part just where he wants it. How strange a body would be if it had only one part! Yes, there are many parts, but only one body. The eye can never say to the hand, "I don't need you." The head can't say to the feet, "I don't need you."*

(1 Corinthians 12:18-21)

Adonijah was fixated on being King, instead of fixating on the perfect plan and timing of the King of Kings to promote him, raise him up, and bless him with influence.

3. CHALLENGE YOURSELF.

If your spiritual father doesn't challenge you in your decisions, your faith, and your personal disciplines, you've got to do it yourself!

I remember actually telling my wife once that I wanted to be in an environment where we weren't big fish in a little pond. We wanted to be pushed and disciplined, not just praised.

That was probably the dumbest prayer I could have prayed, because our next season was one of the most difficult times we've ever had in ministry. We went from being the most praised on a small staff to being at the bottom of the barrel at a mega church. But I know I would not be where I'm at today if I hadn't positioned myself in an environment of discipline.

One of the greatest strengths that we can possess as spiritual sons is self-discipline: discipline in money, discipline in our devotions, discipline in our thought life (especially in terms of lust), and discipline over our bodies.

4. LISTEN TO THE HOLY SPIRIT.

You may not be being challenged by your spiritual father, but it's still your responsibility to be a great man of God. And the best news is we have the Holy Spirit, who doesn't condemn us but convicts us to develop our character and integrity.

I can remember countless times that I may not have had a spiritual father reprimand or challenge me in an area, but the Holy Spirit has. He has told me when I've blown it with my wife. He has told me "Yes, everyone may have liked that message and laughed, but I was grieved." *Ouch!* The Holy Spirit has told me, "It's not the right season to push that topic." In fact, this book wasn't written sooner because I felt the Holy Spirit say, "Wait." And I'm thankful He did.

I suggest you stop now and ask the Holy Spirit to not only guide you, but to help you with any attitudes or mindsets that maybe keeping you from the full purpose of God being fulfilled in your life. He is faithful to answer your prayers.

A FINAL WORD ON PROMOTION

I want to encourage you that if you feel forgotten or overlooked in ministry, God sees you and remembers your desires.

Remember, God is never mocked, so if you are sowing humility and submission, you will reap the results. Trust the process. Don't circumvent what God is doing in your life by trying to expedite His timing. Your best days are ahead. If you are going through a challenging circumstance, realize it is only a test...pass it!

CHAPTER NINE

NAMED BUT NEVER NOTICED

Over the past few chapters, we have journeyed through the lives of four of the 20 sons of David. Despite having the DNA of a legendary King and warrior, an incredible inheritance in both the natural and the spiritual, and having all the resources in the world available to them to become great men of God, Amnon, Absalom, Adonijah, and Chileab all fell short of their purpose and destiny.

While studying these sons, I found a great number of resources and seemingly endless research about their stories, their lives, and their shortcomings. We know about them because they had a story to be told. Whether good or bad, there was something to say.

This next chapter is about the 13 sons of David that have no story, who failed to leave their legacy and failed to leave their mark on the world, in the Kingdom of God, and on eternity.

These are the sons of David who were born in Hebron:

The oldest was Amnon, whose mother was Ahinoam from Jezreel.

The second was Daniel, whose mother was Abigail from Carmel.

The third was Absalom, whose mother was Maacah, the daughter of Talmai, King of Geshur.

The fourth was Adonijah, whose mother was Haggith.

The fifth was Shephatiah, whose mother was Abital.

The sixth was Ithream, whose mother was Eglah, David's wife.

These six sons were born to David in Hebron, where he reigned seven and a half years.

Then David reigned another thirty-three years in Jerusalem. The sons born to David in Jerusalem included Shammua, Shobab, Nathan, and Solomon. Their mother was Bathsheba, the daughter of Ammiel. David also had nine other sons: Ibhar, Elishua, Elpelet, Nogah, Nepheg, Japhia, Elishama, Eliada, and Eliphelet.

These were the sons of David, not including his sons born to his concubines. Their sister was named Tamar.

(1 Chronicles 1:3-9)

Shephatiah, Ithream, Shammua, Shobab, Ibhar, Elishua, Elpelet, Nogah, Nepheg, Japhia, Elishama, Eliada, and Eliphelet were all sons of David, yet we know nothing about them, not their strengths or weaknesses, their accomplishments or failures, or their legacies in Israel. Scripture mentions their name, and nothing more.

No battles won.

No Kingdoms ruled.

No land taken.

Nothing built.

Nothing left.

What did the sons miss? They didn't leave their mark.

MAKE A MARK

It takes intentionality to make a mark, something I learned way back in high school.

When I was a senior, my basketball team played a game in the Seattle Colosseum right before the Sonics played their own game (Yes, the Seattle Supersonics- before the Oklahoma Thunder stole them).

Even though I wasn't exactly a phenomenal basketball player, I wanted to leave my mark in this sport, in the history of Christian Faith High School athletics.

This was my moment—I was in the Seattle Colosseum, playing where my favorite team would be on court in just a matter of hours. So, being a teenager and having pretty oily skin, I schemed to make my mark however I could. While we were doing our layup drill, I made sure I got my greasy fingerprints on the same backboard that Shawn Kemp, Nate McMillan and Gary Payton had touched so many times before.

Those fingerprints boldly declared, Israel Campbell was here, touched this board, and left an impact. I had succeeded—I had left my mark where I wanted to the most that day (Okay, I originally aimed for the rim, but the board was a closer bet.)

My mark may have been small, but my point is, it was *there*. I did something about it, aimed high, and used my resources to do it.

Years later, I had lunch with Bishop TD Jakes, and he told us a powerful story of what his mother told him as a child, a piece of advice that changed his life.

She said, "Teddy, you better leave your mark on this world. I don't care what you have to do—even if it means carving your name into a tree trunk, you better leave your mark!"

I don't know if you know the details of TD Jakes' ministry and life, but he pastors a church of thousands, writes and publishes books, and even makes films. This is a man that has made his mark. I remember this story well—I knew in that moment that I also wanted to leave a legacy that will last.

Oily fingerprints aside, my ultimate purpose and aspiration is to make a mark in the Kingdom of God, to do something that will bring glory to God, affect eternity, and bring many into relationship with Jesus.

I have been a youth pastor in both Seattle and Orlando, and a senior pastor in both North Carolina and Los Angeles. For decades, I've led, taught and pastored hundreds of young men, teenagers, and others in multiple cities and states. In those years, I've experienced challenging relationships, countless late nights of prayer, great obstacles, incredible miracles and many, many victories for the Kingdom of God.

I aim not to just have my ministry be a blip on the screen, but to leave a lasting mark. I aim to make an impact on the lives of others, in guiding, teaching and mentoring them in the Word and the ways of God. It's what I love to do the most, and I believe it's my calling and my destiny.

Ultimately, we are all called to leave our mark. What that might look like depends on what you are called to and how God has gifted you. God does not just tell us what *not* to do—He tells us what to do, to step into our destinies and to bring Him glory.

One of the greatest tragedies for someone that knows God is to simply not leave a mark at all.

WHEN SIN IS NOT WHAT YOU DO, BUT WHAT YOU DON'T DO

In the previous chapters, we've talked about the sins of self-promotion, rebellion, and pride, all of which have resulted in the destruction of destinies and lives.

We might typically think of sin as something intentional, an act. But one definition of sin is "to "miss the mark." Sin can mean to *miss* something as much as it means to do something intentional.

I believe that what I discuss in this chapter is just as deadly as pride or rebelliousness. Theologians call it "the sin of omission": the sin of *not* doing what God has purposed for us.

James 4:17 says,

So whoever knows the right thing to do and fails to do it, for him it is sin.

Rebelling against authority or committing homicide are called sins of commission. They are acts that are *committed* by someone that result in evil, destruction, and go against the will of God. But what happens when someone simply *doesn't* do what they know is right?

If we refuse to feed the hungry, or we don't defend and declare the gospel when it's being attacked, or we withhold generosity or love, we are responsible before God not for what we did do, but for what we didn't.

Jesus gives us a picture of the sin of omission in Luke 10:30-37. He tells the story of a man who has been severely beaten and left on the street to die. Two men pass by him without doing anything. They see his wounds, his helplessness, the fact that he will probably die—and they ignore him. They know what to do to help him and probably save his life. But because of their selfishness or their own agendas or their indifference, they do not stop to care for the man who has been hurt.

One of the most remarkable things about the story of the Good Samaritan is that the two men who passed him should have known better: one was a priest and the other a Temple Assistant, men who would have known that the Word of God instructed them to care for the needy (Deuteronomy 15:11).

I'm sure we've all experienced this to some degree. That twang of regret when we didn't offer prayer to a friend who is hurting, or when we didn't defend Jesus during a conversation that dishonored the truth. Sometimes, it hurts more when we *miss* out on what God has for us than when we know we've committed an act of sin. We know we've "missed the mark"—and missed a key piece of our destiny.

This is what I believe happened to the 13 sons of David who missed the mark.

DESTINY UNFULFILLED

Does it bug anyone else that more than a dozen sons of one of the greatest warriors, leaders, and spiritual fathers of all time, go almost completely unmentioned in the Bible?

Shephatiah, Ithream, Shammua, Shobab, Ibhar, Elishua, Elpelet, Nogah, Nepheg, Japhia, Elishama, Eliada, and Eliphelet were listed in the genealogies of David, but we have no story or other mention of them in the Bible. No Kingdoms they ruled, no buildings they built, no battles they won, no ground taken for Israel. Unlike Amnon, Absalom, and Adonijah, they didn't commit horrendous crimes or twist their identities.

As much as we know, they did nothing horrible—but they didn't do anything great either. Nothing is recorded except their birth, which took a matter of hours and required little effort on their part.

It doesn't take a lot of imagination to think of what these young men *could* have done, with the resources and legacy of their father King David. They could have become great military leaders, spiritual advisors, builders, and advancers of the Kingdom of God. But instead, these sons of David are known simply as names in a list.

Unfortunately, there have been countless spiritual sons with godly, influential spiritual fathers who have missed their destinies not because of what they did, but because of what they didn't do.

Destiny is never handed to you. Destiny has to be acted on.

These 13 sons of David didn't act—and it cost them their destinies. Here are a few theories on what Shephatiah, Ithream, Shammua, Shobab, Ibhar, Elishua, Elpelet, Nogah, Nepheg, Japhia, Elishama, Eliada, and Eliphelet may have missed—and what made them ultimately miss the mark.

1. DON'T SPECTATE... PARTICIPATE.

It can become too easy to simply "watch" the ministries of incredibly gifted spiritual fathers, especially with the accessibility made possible by social media, YouTube, and television. By spectating rather than participating, we learn to passively watch others and not to actively emulate others. Instead of being inspired to leave a mark on this generation, we end up "leaving it to the pros."

It's possible that the 13 destiny-less sons of David found it easier to be impressed by the life of their father than to actually *multiply* his accomplishments. Let's honor and respect the work and the ministries of our spiritual fathers, but also know that we are meant to participate more than spectate.

2. CONVENIENCE CAN KILL.

Unlike their father, these sons of David were raised with the conveniences, luxuries, and opportunities of royalty. They might not have had to fight as hard for their destinies, and as a result, they became lazy. The enemy will often distract us with apathy and indifference order to prevent us from doing anything substantial in the Kingdom. Proverbs 24:33-34 says,

A little extra sleep, a little more slumber, a little folding of the hands to rest—then poverty will pounce on you like a bandit; scarcity will attack you like an armed robber.

Entitlement can come from feeling that everything comes a little too easily—it's possible that these sons didn't take hold of their destinies because it was just a little too convenient.

3. AFRAID TO FAIL?

It must have been pretty intimidating to watch the feats of a father who killed a giant as just a young kid, won incredible military victories, and played the harp and wrote poetry on top of that. It would have been easy to think, *I'll never come close to dad.* But the truth is, the sons of David all had his DNA, and the ability to succeed.

One of the greatest tragedies of this generation is that many people do not know how to pick themselves up again after failing. What we might miss is that victory often only comes after many, many failures. But unfortunately, we don't want to challenge ourselves because of all the "what if's" associated with failing.

What if I'm embarrassed?

What if I lose what I've worked for, or what I already have?

What if I screw up?

Did these sons of David allow these questions to paralyze them, and rob them of leaving their mark?

4. I'M NOT ENOUGH.

One of the key parts of acting on our destinies is knowing our identity. When we don't recognize the authority and the spiritual DNA we carry, we're not walking in our true identities. Instead of knowing we have been chosen, called, and justified for glory (Romans 8:30), we are attacked with thoughts of insignificance.

Just think—each one of the sons of David had to know and compare themselves with each of the other 20. Especially for son #5, or son #12, or son #19, it could have been easy to feel like just another number in a massive lineup.

Likewise, we can easily feel like just another face in the crowd or another body in our church. The enemy would love to get us to settle for anonymity and insignificance—but God has purposed and destined us for influence and impact. Likewise, He must have had more than just a name in a genealogy destined for the sons of David.

5. THEY NEVER MOVED ON.

Scripture says that two of these sons – Shephatiah and Ithream - were born in Hebron instead of Jerusalem. The Kingdom of Israel moved to Jerusalem (2 Samuel 5:6-10), but instead of moving into the future, it's possible that these two sons held onto what was familiar, known, and certain. Hebron was where they were born—it was home. Jerusalem may have seemed uncertain and risky.

Too often, we can hold onto the past because it feels comfortable. We long for the "good old days" and idealize what we've already experienced or known. Technology, methods, and ways change, and if we are unable to embrace progress we could miss out on what God has for us tomorrow, by refusing to alter what feels comfortable and challenging our boundaries.

Could it be possible that these brothers never left their mark because they longed for and idealized the good old days in Hebron? They may not have been willing to move ahead, and it cost them their own futures.

GLORY TO GLORY

Ultimately, we don't know why these sons were never mentioned other than in a genealogy.

But we do know the heart and the mindset of God. He always operates from glory to glory (2 Corinthians 3:18). In other words, He is always multiplying the accomplishments and the advances of the next generation. He does not intend to hide us in obscurity. The Kingdom of God is meant to advance, progress, grow in greatness and glory.

Just look at Scripture:

- After Moses was used by God to deliver his people from Egypt, God used his predecessor Joshua to possess the Promise Land (Joshua).
- Elisha performed double the number of miracles as Elijah (2 Kings 2:9).
- Jesus told His disciples- and us- that we would do even greater miracles than Him (John 14:12).
- Abraham had one son; his son Isaac had two sons; and *his* son Jacob had 12 (Genesis). God multiplies blessings through the generations. That means that each successive generation is meant to receive and multiply the blessings, the inheritance, and the influence of the previous generation.

If our spiritual fathers have accomplished incredible things, then we are meant to multiply those accomplishments! Let's not have the resources and the wisdom from men who slay giants and advance the faith, and just settle for being on the roll call.

Let's receive what has been provided for us by our spiritual fathers, commit to advance the Kingdom of God, and make our mark this generation.

MAKING A MARK, FOR SPIRITUAL SONS

Here are some questions for you to ask yourselves as you reflect on how you are walking out the call of God on your life.

1. What are your sins of omission?
2. What are you intentionally wiping your oily fingers on, or where are you carving your name into the tree?

EMPOWERING THE NEXT GENERATION, FOR SPIRITUAL FATHERS

One of the responsibilities we have as spiritual fathers of the next generation is to empower and teach our spiritual sons to make their own mark.

Here are some questions to ask yourself, as you reflect on how you are mentoring your spiritual sons.

1. What are you specifically imparting to your spiritual sons? How are you instructing them to carry on your own legacy?

2. When was the last time you had a meeting with your spiritual sons where you helped them cast life vision? Ask them, *where are you now in your faith and ministry, and where would you like to be in three years? What about 10 years?*

3. When you are speaking to your spiritual sons, does your tone communicate, "You can do this too," or does it communicate insurmountable challenge and even a lack of faith in ministry?

The biggest tragedy of all might not be a man who screws up his destiny, but a man who completely misses his destiny. As we pursue the call of God to make disciples and advance the Kingdom of God, let's not miss the mark.

CHAPTER TEN

UNNAMED SON

This chapter focuses more on spiritual fathers, but will still be helpful to us all in our pursuit of sonship. It will set us up for success and help us recover and learn from our failures.

There's an incredible amount of pressure on spiritual fathers to uphold integrity and righteousness. Many look to spiritual fathers as role models. They expect and anticipate that they will uphold the word of God not only in their words, but in their actions. It is expected that spiritual fathers will be godly men who will look and act like Christ.

But what if, as spiritual fathers, we blow it? What if we miss the mark, we stumble, we sin?

The sad truth is that many, many spiritual fathers have fallen. In 2 Samuel 11, we read about King David, a spiritual father in the lineage of Christ and a "man after God's own heart" (1 Samuel 13:14).

In the spring of the year, when Kings normally go out to war, David sent Joab and the Israelite army to fight the Ammonites. They destroyed the Ammonite army and laid siege to the city of Rabbah. However, David stayed behind in Jerusalem.

Late one afternoon, after his midday rest, David got out of bed and was walking on the roof of the palace. As he looked out over the city, he noticed a woman of unusual beauty taking a bath. He sent someone to find out who she was, and he was told,

"She is Bathsheba, the daughter of Eliam and the wife of Uriah the Hittite." Then David sent messengers to get her; and when she came to the palace, he slept with her. Later, when Bathsheba discovered that she was pregnant, she sent David a message, saying, "I'm pregnant."

Then David sent word to Joab: "Send me Uriah the Hittite." So Joab sent him to David. When Uriah arrived, David asked him how Joab and the army were getting along and how the war was progressing. Then he told Uriah, "Go on home and relax." David even sent a gift to Uriah after he had left the palace. But Uriah didn't go home. He slept that night at the palace entrance with the King's palace guard.

When David heard that Uriah had not gone home, he summoned him and asked, "What's the matter? Why didn't you go home last night after being away for so long?"

Uriah replied, "The Ark and the armies of Israel and Judah are living in tents, and Joab and my master's men are camping in the open fields. How could I go home to wine and dine and sleep with my wife? I swear that I would never do such a thing."

"Well, stay here today," David told him, "and tomorrow you may return to the army." So Uriah stayed in Jerusalem that day and the next. Then David invited him to dinner and got him drunk. But even then he couldn't get Uriah to go home to his wife. Again he slept at the palace entrance with the King's palace guard.

So the next morning David wrote a letter to Joab and gave it to Uriah to deliver. The letter instructed Joab, "Station Uriah on the front lines where the battle is fiercest. Then pull back so that he will be killed." So Joab assigned Uriah to a spot close to the city wall where he knew the enemy's strongest men were fighting. And when the enemy soldiers came out of the city to fight, Uriah the Hittite was killed along with several other Israelite soldiers.

(2 Samuel 11:1-17)

Not only did David sleep with another man's wife, he arranged for her husband to be killed. That's a double dose of some pretty heavy sin: adultery and homicide in one go. Because he gave in to his flesh, King David fell far, and he fell hard.

To some of us, David's sin might seem inconceivable. It might feel like we could never allow things to get that far.

But are we really so far above David's weakness, his misstep?

Picture this: instead of going to war in the springtime, we stay on the roof. We veer from our purpose, stray from the path. We give in to sin, "crouching at the door" (Genesis 4:7). Or sin crouching on the roof, on our phone and laptop screens, in the congregation in front of us, in the conversations we have with our family, in our thoughts. We miss the mark, and disappoint ourselves and others.

THE WAGES OF SIN

I don't need to tell you that sin is destructive. I'm sure you've experienced the effects of sin in your own life and in the lives of people you know and love. Whether in real life or on the cover of *Us* magazine, we've all seen families, marriages, friendships, and communities destroyed by affairs, addictions, and abuse.

As spiritual fathers, we may not be committing adultery or plotting homicide, but we can "miss the mark" in a number of ways. Maybe you take spiritual pride in your position, harbor insecurity that causes you to manipulate others, or even engage in "church gossip."

I'm not going to list every single way that a spiritual father has missed the mark, but we do need to be aware that pride, lust, and covetousness can creep into our lives barely noticed. I'll trust the Holy Spirit to show us those areas of weakness that may turn to sin, or areas that we are already struggling with sin. He is faithful to convict us, because He wants us to walk in freedom.

When we do miss the mark, we are not the only ones affected by our bad choices and slip-ups. Many others, including our spiritual sons, will suffer the "collateral damage," as shown in the aftermath of David's sin with Bathsheba.

There is always a price to pay for sin.

David's sin resulted not only in the death of Uriah, but ultimately in the death of his firstborn son with Bathsheba.

When we screw up, there is collateral damage to spiritual sons.

In 2 Samuel 11 and 12, we see the aftermath of the messy tangle of sin that David got himself into on the rooftop. After the death of Uriah—at his own hand—David slept with Bathsheba again, and they conceived a son.

> *When Uriah's wife heard that her husband was dead, she mourned for him. When the period of mourning was over, David sent for her and brought her to the palace, and she became one of his wives. Then she gave birth to a son. But the LORD was displeased with what David had done.*
>
> (2 Samuel 11:26-27)

After the prophet Nathan told David a parable to convict him of his sin with Bathsheba, David realized what he had done (see Chapter Five for more details on this exchange).

After Nathan finished his story, David 'fessed up.

> *Then David confessed to Nathan, "I have sinned against the Lord."*
>
> *Nathan replied, "Yes, but the Lord has forgiven you, and you won't die for this sin. Nevertheless, because you have shown utter contempt for the word of the Lord by doing this, your child will die."*
>
> *After Nathan returned to his home, the Lord sent a deadly illness to the child of David and Uriah's wife. David begged God to spare the child. He went without food and lay all night on the bare ground. The elders of his household pleaded with him to get up and eat with them, but he refused.*
>
> *Then on the seventh day the child died. David's advisers were afraid to tell him. "He wouldn't listen to reason while the child was ill," they said. "What drastic thing will he do when we tell him the child is dead?"*
>
> *When David saw them whispering, he realized what had happened. "Is the child dead?" he asked.*
>
> *"Yes," they replied, "he is dead."*
>
> *Then David got up from the ground, washed himself, put on lotions, and changed his clothes. He went to the Tabernacle and*

worshiped the Lord. After that, he returned to the palace and was served food and ate.

His advisers were amazed. "We don't understand you," they told him. "While the child was still living, you wept and refused to eat. But now that the child is dead, you have stopped your mourning and are eating again."

David replied, "I fasted and wept while the child was alive, for I said, 'Perhaps the Lord will be gracious to me and let the child live.' But why should I fast when he is dead? Can I bring him back again? I will go to him one day, but he cannot return to me."

Then David comforted Bathsheba, his wife, and slept with her. She became pregnant and gave birth to a son, and David named him Solomon. The Lord loved the child and sent word through Nathan the prophet that they should name him Jedidiah (which means "beloved of the Lord"), as the Lord had commanded.

(2 Samuel 12:13-25)

Can you imagine how his father felt? King David's grievous sin and rejection of the word of God and the law of God brought about something worse than his own death, as any parent knows. It brought about the death of a child.

David grieved- he wept, prayed, and finally anointed himself. And then he went back to creating new sons to replace the one he so tragically lost.

Sometimes, the damage done to our spiritual sons in the wake of our own sins can look like more than wounded egos and disappointment. In David's case, because he "showed contempt for the word of the Lord," his newborn infant died. His son's destiny and purpose were cut short.

While we do make our own choices on how we respond to the sin and the mistakes of others, as we've discussed in previous chapters, there may be spiritual sons who never recover from witnessing our own struggles with pride, adultery, manipulation, and other ways that we "miss the mark." They may feel betrayed, confused, and let down, or even become disillusioned with the Church.

I have worked at churches with powerful, faith-filled, anointed leaders—and they *still* screwed up. Even while God is at work and using people for His purposes and His Kingdom—like David, I've seen the sin- especially the pride and arrogance- of spiritual fathers cause incredible pain and hurt to others, ultimately causing them to leave the Church. It breaks my heart to see many of those sons of the house no longer in the Church, and worst of all, no longer in love with Jesus. The drama and "prophetic" manipulation they witnessed caused them to resent their churches and their church leadership. They've abdicated their callings as leaders and influencers in the Kingdom of God, robbing themselves (and us) of their destinies.

Much like the unnamed son of David and Bathsheba who died as an infant, it is as if they've never lived.

It may feel like a lot of pressure to put on us as spiritual fathers to know that our choices can affect the destinies of others. The reality is that our personal walks with Christ become more than just "about us" when we are fathering and mentoring others to know and walk with the Lord.

The Bible instructs spiritual fathers this way:

> *If anyone wants to provide leadership in the church, good! But there are preconditions: A leader must be well-thought-of, committed to his wife, cool and collected, accessible, and hospitable. He must know what he's talking about, not be overfond of wine, not pushy but gentle, not thin-skinned, not money-hungry. He must handle his own affairs well, attentive to his own children and having their respect. For if someone is unable to handle his own affairs, how can he take care of God's church? He must not be a new believer, lest the position go to his head and the Devil trip him up. Outsiders must think well of him, or else the Devil will figure out a way to lure him into his trap.*

(1 Timothy 3:1-7 MSG)

There are a lot of expectations for being a leader in the church, including conditions that not only speak to our personal faith, but the way our lives look from the outside. Why so many preconditions to being a spiritual father?

Here's why: our good or bad conduct affects more than just us. Our behavior impacts our families, the church, the community, and those we lead, including our spiritual sons.

HOW WE RESPOND MEANS EVERYTHING

If we know Jesus, we strive to lead and to live without sinning. But when we've fallen short—and we know it—what do we do in response? How do we repent and come back into right standing with God, ourselves, and others?

Even though King David royally screwed up, he still responded to his sin in the right way. David may have fallen far, and missed the mark by a mile, but he still went on to be recorded in the Word of God as one of the greatest spiritual fathers in history (even Jesus Himself was called "Son of David").

So, how did David respond when he realized he had sinned, and how can we learn from his example? In other words, what do we do when we screw up?

1. ADMIT OUR FAULTS.

I love that David eventually admitted his sin (2 Samuel 12:13), even after having to be confronted with a parable to understand just what he did. As a spiritual father, one of the most powerful things we can ever do to lead others is to admit our own faults and weaknesses.

In Bible College, one of my professors taught that as a man of God or as a pastor, you must never show your weaknesses your faults to the people you are leading. I remember thinking to myself, *I don't ever want to be that kind of leader.*

I want to be a leader that people can relate to, a leader that people know is authentic, honest, and working through things just like everybody else. I admit that I have faults and weaknesses, even as I set an example of integrity and am able to say, "Follow my example, as I follow the example of Christ" (1 Corinthians 11:1 NIV).

When David committed adultery with Bathsheba, my guess is that all of Jerusalem already knew about it. I'm sure there were whispers and gossip circulating through the streets and marketplaces like wildfire.

Did you hear about King David and the wife of Uriah? Is it true—could our King do this?

The people under the leadership of King David may have felt hurt, betrayed, and confused. Only when David admitted he had sinned, could healing and restoration for everyone impacted by his sin begin.

2. FIGHT FOR OUR SPIRITUAL SONS.

When David's infant son fell ill because of his own sin, he pleaded with the Lord and fasted for days (2 Samuel 12:16-17). Here was a father aware of his own mistake and desperate for his child to live, taking action and doing whatever he could to remedy the situation. As spiritual fathers, we have to intercede for our sons who have and are currently dying in the wake of our mistakes. We have to become aware of those who are no longer thriving or who are barely making it as a part of the collateral damage from our own sin, and we must plead with and seek God on their behalf.

David wasn't praying for himself, or to be forgiven. He was praying for the destiny of his son to be preserved.

3. DECLARE WHO WE ARE IN CHRIST.

One of my favorite moments in the Bible is when David anointed himself, although he had already been anointed by Samuel (1 Samuel 16:13), the leaders in Hebron (2 Samuel 5:3), the entire nation of Israel (2 Samuel 5:3), and in Psalm 23 in the presence of his enemies (Psalm 23:5). David was anointed again and again throughout Scripture, reaffirming his "God identity" and "God destiny."

After he sinned, he anointed himself again.

It's so important that we are strong enough not to wallow in shame, but to declare our righteousness in Christ. As Paul said in the letter to the Philippians:

No, dear brothers and sisters, I have not achieved it, but I focus on this one thing: Forgetting the past and looking forward to what lies ahead

(Philippians 3:13)

We may have sinned. We may have let pride slip in, led others by manipulation, or slipped up in a relationship. Once we repent, we've got to anoint ourselves, as it says in Psalm 92:10 (KJV):

But my horn shalt thou exalt like the horn of a unicorn: I shall be anointed with fresh oil.

It's a new day and a new season. Let's press ahead, regardless of the circumstances. Our spiritual sons - and others - need us to! Let's learn to anoint ourselves afresh again and stand firm on our identities.

4. PRODUCE MORE SONS.

2 Samuel 12:24 says that David comforted Bathsheba after the death of their firstborn, and she birthed another son—Solomon, who would become one of the greatest Kings of all time.

Despite our failures and mistakes, God wants us to produce more sons. We are told to populate the earth, not just with physical children, but with spiritual children. Jesus told his disciples to reproduce more disciples in the Great Commission:

Therefore, go and make disciples of all the nations, baptizing them in the name of the Father and the Son and the Holy Spirit. Teach these new disciples to obey all the commands I have given you. And be sure of this: I am with you always, even to the end of the age.

(Matthew 28:19-20)

We must continue to mentor, guide, lead, instruct and rebuke as needed. Don't let your failure of yesterday keep you from bringing much-needed wisdom to the next generation of sons. They desperately need you to fulfill your destiny and purpose and your guidance to fulfill destiny and to continue advancing the Kingdom of God!

Maybe you are that son who was taken out by the collateral damage of a spiritual father. I don't believe that it's an accident that you are reading this book.

Your spiritual father (or earthly father) may have hurt you beyond what you feel can be healed or restored. You may have experienced great pain and disillusionment, or betrayal. But I know this: your heavenly Father wants to heal and restore you.

Remember that the enemy often attacks us in our infancy. When Moses was a child, Pharaoh tried to kill all the Hebrew boys (Exodus 1:16) and when Jesus was a baby, Herod tried to kill all the baby boys born in Bethlehem (Matthew 2:16). Neither were successful from stunting the plan of God, but there was a premeditated effort to take out men of God (and in the case of Jesus, the Son of God Himself).

The enemy may try to take you out in your infancy because he knows you are called to be a deliverer. Don't let the enemy win! Return to God and what He says about you, reestablish your relationship with Jesus, and let the Holy Spirit once again lead you to a church where you can be planted and once again become a spiritual son.

Sin is ugly, and can cause great damage, and even death. But its power and hold are not beyond the redemptive power of the blood of Jesus, and the goodness and mercy of God.

CHAPTER ELEVEN
SOLOMON UNOFFENDED

One of the greatest abilities we can develop as spiritual sons is the ability to remain unoffended.

I know what you're about to say—

But Pastor Israel ...

He insulted me behind my back.

She's not submitting to my leadership.

He stole my seat in church.

I hear you. In most cases, your pain and hurt are valid when someone insults you. Someone may have insulted you unjustly, embarrassed you, or hurt the people you love. He or she may have stolen from you, tried to undermine who you are, or even brought dishonor on the name of Jesus.

Unfortunately, the devil will use this opportunity to stick it to us. He wants to cause division and strife with others and to keep us mired in unforgiveness. Jesus said that "the thief's purpose is to steal and kill and destroy," but that He came "to give [you] a rich and satisfying life" (John 10:10). We can allow the enemy to steal from us, or we can choose what Christ gives us: an abundant life fully of mercy and grace.

The key to remaining rooted in your purpose and destiny regardless of what others do to you is *not to hold onto offense*. No matter how much it hurts.

Why?

Because holding onto offense ultimately hurts you more than the original act, remark, or behavior ever could.

In the age of social media, it's easy to respond immediately to a comment, post, or video that we find hurtful with tears, outrage, and more insults. Anytime anyone says something we don't like or we don't approve of, we have 280 characters we can vent with on Twitter.

As a culture, we have become a bunch of babies when it comes to the actions, opinions, and beliefs of others. We have become so preoccupied with being politically correct that we feel insulted at anything and everything that expresses a slightly different viewpoint than our own. We even get offended if people are offended by us. I am not saying that we should approve of abuse, but we are facing a crisis of over-protection and sensitivity. We don't teach grit.

The problem with staying offended is that we don't have the *right* to be offended. Why? Because more than any other human that ever existed, Jesus had the right to be offended. He was mocked, ostracized, betrayed, insulted, gossiped about, criticized, beaten, and ultimately killed for *teaching the truth.*

He is God, and He remained unoffended, when we mocked Him, spit on Him, and crucified Him. Given His example, we do not have the right to choose offense- ever. He has chosen to be unoffended by us, continually offering us grace and mercy.

There's another man in the Bible who showed us a good example of not being offended. This guy took the high road in every situation, even when he was insulted and treated unjustly. If any man in the Old Testament had the right to be offended, it was Solomon, the second son of David and Bathsheba.

SOLOMON, UNOFFENDED

May I suggest that Solomon's greatest attribute wasn't wisdom?

The Bible says that was known to be "wiser than anyone else" (1 Kings 4:31), but I believe there is a significant aspect to his wisdom that we often overlook. It is part of the reason he asked for wisdom from God in the first place (1 Kings 3:9).

Solomon had the humility to ask for wisdom because he remained unoffended by the actions of those he loved the most. The problem is, many people never make it to asking for guidance and wisdom because they are too caught up in their own unforgiveness, vindictiveness, and offense against other people. They are too preoccupied to even have the wherewithal to ask for wisdom.

Let's put ourselves in Solomon's shoes for a second.

When Solomon was growing up, I am sure people whispered and made comments about him and his family. If he were to live in this generation, there would have been teachers who would have told him that he would never amount to anything in his life. The kids on the playground would have spread rumors of his father's track record. He probably heard endless whispers and gossip about his birth, withstood insults, and maybe even mockery.

After all, his own father seduced his mother out of wedlock (some might even say he raped her). Then he tried to hide it and even had his mother's first husband killed.

Solomon must have known all this, and yet somehow, he never got offended. Somehow, he doesn't let this affect his relationship with his father David.

Solomon eventually inherited the Kingdom of Israel because he remained loyal to his father. While some of the other sons of David that we've seen rebelled (Absalom) and ran (Amnon) from King David, Solomon never tried to usurp his authority, or criticize him for his actions.

We also see biblical evidence that Solomon interacted with people who had offended him with patience and forgiveness. He didn't just deal with hurt well; he made decisions based on peace and justice, rather than on his own emotions.

As we read about in Chapter Eight, Adonijah tried to promote himself to King, even though King David had promised Bathsheba that Solomon would sit on the throne. Remember? Adonijah threw himself a big party to declare himself King of Israel. He was having a great time until a big downer showed up to spoil the party. His friend

Jonathan, son of Abiathar, arrived to tell him the news that Adonijah's brother Solomon had been declared King.

> *And while he was still speaking, Jonathan son of Abiathar the priest arrived.*
>
> *"Come in," Adonijah said to him, "for you are a good man. You must have good news."*
>
> *"Not at all!" Jonathan replied. "Our lord King David has just declared Solomon King! The King sent him down to Gihon Spring with Zadok the priest, Nathan the prophet, and Benaiah son of Jehoiada, protected by the King's bodyguard. They had him ride on the King's own mule, and Zadok and Nathan have anointed him at Gihon Spring as the new King. They have just returned, and the whole city is celebrating and rejoicing. That's what all the noise is about.*
>
> (1 Kings 1:42-45)

Even though Adonijah usurped David's authority by declaring himself King of Israel, Solomon didn't get offended that his brother did what he did. Instead, he remained cool and collected. He didn't overreact.

> *Then all of Adonijah's guests jumped up in panic from the banquet table and quickly scattered. Adonijah was afraid of Solomon, so he rushed to the sacred tent and grabbed on to the horns of the altar. Word soon reached Solomon that Adonijah had seized the horns of the altar in fear, and that he was pleading, "Let King Solomon swear today that he will not kill me!"*
>
> *Solomon replied, "If he proves himself to be loyal, not a hair on his head will be touched. But if he makes trouble, he will die." So King Solomon summoned Adonijah, and they brought him down from the altar. He came and bowed respectfully before King Solomon, who dismissed him, saying, "Go on home."*
>
> (1 Kings 1:49-53)

Adonijah expected Solomon to slice his head off, but he didn't lift a finger. Instead, he said, "go home"—he released him completely, despite the fact that his own brother tried to steal his right and his greatest gift: Kingship.

Solomon also showed this incredible ability to remain unoffended when dealing with Shimei. Shimei was a man from the clan of Saul, who vengefully attacked King David by throwing rocks (and insults) when David came into his village.

> As King David came to Bahurim, a man came out of the village cursing them. It was Shimei son of Gera, from the same clan as Saul's family. He threw stones at the King and the King's officers and all the mighty warriors who surrounded him. "Get out of here, you murderer, you scoundrel!" he shouted at David. "The LORD is paying you back for all the bloodshed in Saul's clan. You stole his throne, and now the LORD has given it to your son Absalom. At last you will taste some of your own medicine, for you are a murderer!"
>
> (2 Samuel 16:5-8)

In light of what Shimei did to his father, Solomon should have been incredibly offended at this man. He easily could have had him killed on the spot. But instead, he refused to be offended, and gave him a lenient sentence:

> The King then sent for Shimei and told him, "Build a house here in Jerusalem and live there. But don't step outside the city to go anywhere else. On the day you so much as cross the Kidron Valley, you will surely die; and your blood will be on your own head."
>
> Shimei replied, "Your sentence is fair; I will do whatever my lord the King commands." So Shimei lived in Jerusalem for a long time.
>
> (1 Kings 2:36-38)

Unfortunately, Shimei eventually took advantage of Solomon's generosity and was killed.

> Solomon heard that Shimei had left Jerusalem and had gone to Gath and returned. So the King sent for Shimei and demanded, "Didn't I make you swear by the LORD and warn you not to go anywhere else or you would surely die? And you replied, 'The sentence is fair; I will do as you say.' Then why haven't you kept your oath to the LORD and obeyed my command?"

The King also said to Shimei, "You certainly remember all the wicked things you did to my father, David. May the LORD now bring that evil on your own head. But may I, King Solomon, receive the LORD's blessings, and may one of David's descendants always sit on this throne in the presence of the LORD." Then, at the King's command, Benaiah son of Jehoiada took Shimei outside and killed him.

So the Kingdom was now firmly in Solomon's grip.

(1 Kings 2:41-46)

In all of these situations, we see that Solomon cultivated an incredible ability to not hold onto offense—and he saw the fruit. He ruled as King, and eventually was able to complete the destiny and purpose begun by His father.

I believe that the ability to not get offended was part of the root of Solomon's legendary wisdom, and why he went down in history as one of the greatest Kings of all time and one of the heroes of the Bible. It was this ability that allowed him to succeed where so many of David's other sons failed.

Being able to remain unoffended regardless of the situation is not a divine gift or talent. It is something we can all cultivate. The ability to release anger and to show mercy and grace is a choice that will produce great fruit in our lives if we allow it to.

HOW TO LIVE AN UNOFFENDABLE LIFE

Solomon didn't just live an unoffended life, he taught it. It was crucial for him that he passed this key onto the next generation.

Take a look at the following proverbs, which Solomon wrote.

Whoever covers an offense seeks love, but he who repeats a matter separates close friends.

(Proverbs 17:9 ESV)

Good sense makes one slow to anger, and it is his glory to overlook an offense.

(Proverbs 19:11 ESV)

Solomon's words were rooted in his own experience, and have been included in Scripture as the infallible Word of God. This should make us stop and think: we have to take this issue very, very seriously. Being a son of the promise is being someone who chooses to see the good in his father no matter what the crowd is whispering. Solomon saw the weaknesses of his father David—and even experienced the repercussions of his sin—and he still supported and honored him.

Too often when we see the flaws of our spiritual fathers, we pack up and go looking for a new spiritual father. We get offended by their weaknesses and poor decisions, only to disqualify ourselves from receiving our inheritance. I see this pattern too often in the Body of Christ today, and I believe it's stunting the growth of not only individuals but of the Church.

We've all been hurt—and if you're a Christian it's likely that you've been hurt in churches by mentors or spiritual fathers. And if you haven't been wounded, insulted, or abused yet, prepare yourself: the Bible says surely offense will come (Luke 17:1).

If offense is inevitable, we've got to be prepared and equipped on how to handle it so that we can overcome. We can't allow Satan to trap us in this snare.

If you take anything away from this book, hear me on this one thing: *How you handle offense will determine your future.*

If you can remain unoffended, no matter the insults, abuse, or injustices that come your way, you will be promoted, and eventually, you may do even more than your spiritual father.

I know this may seem easier said than done. I don't know your story, and you may have gone through horrible abuse and betrayal, even from other Christians. I'm betting I have a few stories in my personal life that could hang next to yours.

But this isn't a comparison game of *who has suffered more?* This is a lesson of *don't let the past and the pain rob you of who God has called you to be.*

Be a spiritual son that doesn't get offended. Be a spiritual son who does the things that the Davids never did—like Solomon, who finished building the Temple. Let's go even farther than our spiritual fathers by remaining unoffendable.

Here are seven keys to remaining unoffended, no matter what comes our way.

1. GET IN THE WORD.

The Bible says, *Great peace have they which love thy law: and nothing shall offend them.*
(Psalm 119:165 KJV)

I've found an incredible correlation between my own personal Bible study time and my ability to keep from being offended. Yep, I know that's old school....but it's true. The more of the Word I have in me, the less carnal and emotional and "It's about me" mentality I have.

If you are having a hard time dealing with your spiritual father, take a look at your devotional life- is it high or running on empty? Most of the time, the more easily you are offended, the less time you are spending in the Bible. I'm not talking about podcasts, or prepping for a sermon, or your Bethel station on Pandora. I'm talking about your heavenly Father talking to you through his Word and the Holy Spirit.

2. GUARD YOUR EARS.

Who are you listening to?

An offended friend, church member, or even wife can cause us to get offended over something that was never directed at us in the first place. That's why I'm saying don't just guard your heart—guard your ears.

I don't know how many times I've seen spiritual sons get offended by something their spiritual fathers *did not even* do to them. Somehow what a leader or mentor did to someone else (usually retold with bias) produces resentment, frustration, strife, envy, and finally offense in an onlooker.

Be careful of who is feeding your information intake, even with a couple comments here and a couple sarcastic remarks there. This will only feed offense in the speaker and the listener. When you give an offense fuel, it is a hard weed to get rid of that can choke out your future.

3. SET BOUNDARIES.

Not a real popular word right now, and not a word I love, but I think is applicable in this context. Sometimes we don't want to be told what's good for us and what's bad for us. But *boundaries* are key for our success.

Sometimes we get offended because we never established boundaries for ourselves, and then got worn out and hurt when too much has been asked of us, especially in ministry. Many times, I see spiritual sons that are actually responsible for their own offense, because they never raised their hand and said "I need help" or "I can't keep up at that pace." They got offended that their spiritual fathers didn't realize they were struggling, yet there had never been any critical conversations (see Chapter Five on "crucial conversations").

We are responsible for our own spiritual health. We cannot blame others, including our spiritual fathers, for not creating for our own boundaries for keeping an unoffended heart. Solomon gave Shimei boundaries that he violated.

4. KEEP YOUR VISION FRESH.

Offense is like the rewind button on an old VCR (if you're under the age of 18, sorry for the archaic reference). Dwelling on how you've been offended keeps you stuck in the past.

Keep fresh vision for your future in front of you. What words have been spoken over you? What do you dream of doing for the Kingdom of God? If you have a big vision, then little hiccups won't upset you. If you've got a small vision then every tiny offense, insult, or jab seems huge.

Remember, God has great plans for your life (Jeremiah 29:11). These plans shouldn't be stunted by your own insecurity and unforgiveness. David couldn't build the Temple because he had blood on his hands (1 Chronicles 22:8). Solomon stayed unoffended, kept blood off his hands, and did what the famous King David could never do. Look towards your future, not your past hurts that keep you mired in offense.

5. BE THE FIRST TO DROP YOUR STONE.

Remember the story of Jesus:

> *As he was speaking, the teachers of religious law and the Pharisees brought a woman who had been caught in the act of adultery. They put her in front of the crowd.*
>
> *"Teacher," they said to Jesus, "this woman was caught in the act of adultery. The law of Moses says to stone her. What do you say?"*
>
> *They were trying to trap him into saying something they could use against him, but Jesus stooped down and wrote in the dust with his finger. They kept demanding an answer, so he stood up again and said, "All right, but let the one who has never sinned throw the first stone!" Then he stooped down again and wrote in the dust.*
>
> *When the accusers heard this, they slipped away one by one, beginning with the oldest, until only Jesus was left in the middle of the crowd with the woman.*
>
> (John 8:3-9)

Notice the older and wiser men dropped their stone first.

If you've *never* in your life done *anything* that would cause someone to be offended, then go ahead and be offended. But we all know that we have sinned against ourselves and others. Be the first to drop the stone.

6. WE CAN BE RIGHT- AND STILL BE WRONG.

When we are hurt or insulted, we might be right to think what that person has done is wrong. **But,** we are wrong when we remain offended. Enough said.

7. **Allow the Holy Spirit to do His job.**

Allow the Holy Spirit to show your spiritual father his own issues, if he is the one who offended you. I promise you that God will convict him. Your spiritual father didn't get as far as he has without listening to the Holy Spirit...even if he's stubborn and usually doesn't admit when he is wrong. I've noticed that if I just keep my heart right, the Holy Spirit will keep my spiritual father's heart right!

Listen to David's final words to Solomon:

As the time of King David's death approached, he gave this charge to his son Solomon:

"I am going where everyone on earth must someday go. Take courage and be a man. Observe the requirements of the LORD your God, and follow all his ways. Keep the decrees, commands, regulations, and laws written in the Law of Moses so that you will be successful in all you do and wherever you go. If you do this, then the LORD will keep the promise he made to me. He told me, 'If your descendants live as they should and follow me faithfully with all their heart and soul, one of them will always sit on the throne of Israel.'

(1 Kings 2:1-4)

If we can keep from getting offended, we will position ourselves for incredible blessings from our spiritual fathers: gifts of leadership, authority, and great purpose and destiny.

CHAPTER TWELVE

FINISHING THE RACE

In 2006, I ran the New York Marathon. I started strong, but around mile 18, I hit a wall. I was pounding the pavement, sweat pouring down, thinking about that cheeseburger at the end of the race, when I started to become delusional. *I have to be close to the end*, I thought—*around mile 23 at least*. But once I spotted the markers, I saw I was still *eight miles* away from the finish line...eight more miles of grueling concrete.

I thought, *there's no way. Am I being punk'd?*

Someone must be moving the mile markers to trick the runners.

Unfortunately, I was wrong. I was only on mile 18, far from the finish line, and couldn't blame anyone else for how tired/impatient I felt, how much my body hurt, and how far away I was from that juicy double cheeseburger. So, I ended up walking...until I reached downtown, where onlookers were packed along the sidelines, cheering us on.

This is where I wanted to show the crowd - and my own kids, who were waiting to watch me pass - that I wasn't struggling. I wanted to show them I had stores of energy...could have run a second marathon if I needed to! I didn't want them to see that their dad wasn't the Usain Bolt they might have imagined. So, I started to run again.

The crowd only saw "my best," but if you followed the pace tracker on my shoe you would have seen the part where I wasn't doing so good: the moments where I faltered, second guessed myself, and slowed way, way down.

The great thing about the Bible is that when it tells the story of Solomon, it lists not only the good but the bad. We read about his moments that make us cheer *and* his moments that make us cringe and even feel disappointed.

In the previous chapter, we saw a Solomon that set an incredible example for us: he saw the rewards of being unoffendable by becoming a great leader and the wisest man on Earth. But sadly, in the book of Ecclesiastes, we see a Solomon that fell victim to the meaninglessness of life, a Solomon that made mistake after mistake and eventually abdicated his destiny.

And as disappointed as we might be from Solomon's mistakes and eventual downfall, these Scriptures help us learn to avoid his mistakes in our own lives, so that we can finish the race well.

ALL IS MEANINGLESS

The Solomon in Ecclesiastes was a different man than the one we saw in the previous chapter. Solomon became discouraged. He became disillusioned. He lost purpose, and became blind to life's meaning and purpose. Because of his great wisdom, he was still called "The Teacher" but his perspective was of a man who lost hope.

"Everything is meaningless," says the Teacher, "completely meaningless!"

What do people get for all their hard work under the sun? Generations come and generations go, but the earth never changes. The sun rises and the sun sets, then hurries around to rise again. The wind blows south, and then turns north. Around and around it goes, blowing in circles. Rivers run into the sea, but the sea is never full. Then the water returns again to the rivers and flows out again to the sea. Everything is wearisome beyond description. No matter how much we see, we are never satisfied. No matter how much we hear, we are not content.

(Ecclesiastes 1:2-8)

Could it be that Solomon came to this conclusion during the process of his own personal downfall?

In the previous chapter, we saw a ruler and a King with a great destiny before him. But somewhere along the way, he lost his way. And it started with allowing his heart to be turned by all of his wives, the very thing God had warned about.

> *Now King Solomon loved many foreign women. Besides Pharaoh's daughter, he married women from Moab, Ammon, Edom, Sidon, and from among the Hittites. The* Lord *had clearly instructed the people of Israel, "You must not marry them, because they will turn your hearts to their gods." Yet Solomon insisted on loving them anyway. He had 700 wives of royal birth and 300 concubines. And in fact, they did turn his heart away from the* Lord.
>
> *In Solomon's old age, they turned his heart to worship other gods instead of being completely faithful to the* Lord *his God, as his father, David, had been. Solomon worshiped Ashtoreth, the goddess of the Sidonians, and Molech, the detestable god of the Ammonites. In this way, Solomon did what was evil in the* Lord's *sight; he refused to follow the* Lord *completely, as his father, David, had done.*
>
> *On the Mount of Olives, east of Jerusalem, he even built a pagan shrine for Chemosh, the detestable god of Moab, and another for Molech, the detestable god of the Ammonites. Solomon built such shrines for all his foreign wives to use for burning incense and sacrificing to their gods.*
>
> *The* Lord *was very angry with Solomon, for his heart had turned away from the* Lord, *the God of Israel, who had appeared to him twice. He had warned Solomon specifically about worshiping other gods, but Solomon did not listen to the* Lord's *command. So now the* Lord *said to him, "Since you have not kept my covenant and have disobeyed my decrees, I will surely tear the Kingdom away from you and give it to one of your servants. But for the sake of your father, David, I will not do this while you are still alive. I will take the Kingdom away from your son. And even so, I will not take away the entire Kingdom; I will let him*

be King of one tribe, for the sake of my servant David and for the sake of Jerusalem, my chosen city."

(1 Kings 11:1-13 NKJV)

Solomon threw away his destiny and his purpose by sowing his wild oats and chasing tail. Instead of getting better with age, Solomon actually got worse. The consequences of this "turning" were disastrous. He began to worship other gods, building pricey shrines for them. He turned from the Lord, the One who had given him great wisdom and incredible blessing.

The biggest tragedy might be that his own kids ended up worse than him. We are supposed to exceed the accomplishments of our fathers and to build on their foundations, just like Solomon had done with the Temple. But Solomon let his foundations splinter and allowed the inheritance of his children to fall through the cracks.

Not only were his children affected, the Kingdom of Israel was actually split in two. It was meant to enter into an era of great peace and prosperity, but the Lord "[tore] the Kingdom away from [Solomon]" because he worshipped other gods.

Solomon's inheritance from his father David before him ended up in a constant cycle of disobedience and exile, as the people of Israel would enter centuries of turmoil.

Solomon screwed up, affecting his kids, his kids' kids, and an entire nation.

Are you depressed yet?

Fortunately, we learn a valuable lesson from Solomon's story. We learn the value of obeying specific principles that are explicitly laid out by the Word of God, Scripture that Solomon would have read himself.

In the book of Deuteronomy, we are given four principles for a King to obey, rules that would have helped Solomon to finish the race strong if he had followed them. They are also principles that will help us finish strong as spiritual sons, so that we can pass the Kingdom on to the next generation stronger and more powerful than how it was passed on to us.

In the following passage, Moses dictated to the Israelites precepts for entering the Promise Land successfully—to step into the inheritance that God had promised them with longevity. It also set a precedent for all Kings to follow.

> *"When you come to the land that the LORD your God is giving you, and you possess it and dwell in it and then say, 'I will set a King over me, like all the nations that are around me,' you may indeed set a King over you whom the LORD your God will choose. One from among your brothers you shall set as King over you. You may not put a foreigner over you, who is not your brother. Only he must not acquire many horses for himself or cause the people to return to Egypt in order to acquire many horses, since the LORD has said to you, 'You shall never return that way again.' And he shall not acquire many wives for himself, lest his heart turn away, nor shall he acquire for himself excessive silver and gold.*
>
> *"And when he sits on the throne of his Kingdom, he shall write for himself in a book a copy of this law, approved by the Levitical priests. And it shall be with him, and he shall read in it all the days of his life, that he may learn to fear the LORD his God by keeping all the words of this law and these statutes, and doing them, that his heart may not be lifted up above his brothers, and that he may not turn aside from the commandment, either to the right hand or to the left, so that he may continue long in his Kingdom, he and his children, in Israel.*
>
> (Deuteronomy 17:1-20)

Scripture contains definite rules for how the Kingdom should be ruled: by a leader who is radically devoted to God, his heart wholly turned to the Lord. Likewise, as spiritual sons and leaders in our own right, we must ask ourselves if we are following the same principles of obedience, devotion, and commitment to the Lord.

Here are four basic principles to obey to make sure that unlike Solomon, we finish the race well.

1. DON'T GO BACK TO EGYPT.

> *Only he must not acquire many horses for himself or cause the people **to return to Egypt** in order to acquire many horses, since the Lord has said to you, 'You shall never return that way again.'*

Isn't it interesting that the first wife of Solomon was an Egyptian?

Solomon made an alliance with Pharaoh, the King of Egypt, and married one of his daughters. He brought her to live in the City of David until he could finish building his palace and the Temple of the LORD and the wall around the city.

(1 Kings 3:1)

In a sense, the first rule was "Don't go back to Egypt."

The first rule Solomon broke as King was to marry Pharaoh's daughter, and align himself to Egypt. For the nation of Israel, Egypt represented bondage. It was the place they had been delivered from, a place of slavery and repression.

As spiritual sons, I think a very good "benchmark" or rule we should try to follow is:

Does this or can this take me back into bondage?

You might not think this applies to you, but most of us have an "Egypt" in our lives, a place where we might find ourselves trapped, repressed, and back into sin.

It might not be a popular message to avoid specific temptations— but sin "easily entangles" when we give it the opportunity (Hebrews 12:1 NIV). In the passage in Deuteronomy, the Word warned Kings not to go backwards or connect themselves to things that used to keep them in bondage. I've seen way too many sons who have been set free by the power of the Holy Spirit then lower their guard, and slowly but surely become bound to the same strongholds all over again.

I'm not going to try to be the Holy Spirit and give you a list of "bondages." I trust that the Holy Spirit will convict, teach, and transform you and give you the ability to finish strong.

Unfortunately, in the era of the "grace" message, people like to use the mercy and forgiveness of God as license to do what they want, without worrying about restrictions.

The Apostle Paul said,

You say, "I am allowed to do anything"—but not everything is good for you. You say, "I am allowed to do anything"—but not everything is beneficial.

(1 Corinthians 10:23)

Before engaging in an activity or going somewhere that might be risky for you, ask yourself:

Does this or can this take me back into bondage?

2. MAKE YOUR MARRIAGE THE BEST IT CAN BE.

"And he shall not acquire many wives for himself, lest his heart turn away."

The second thing that the passage instructed Kings to avoid were "many wives"—a rule broken by Solomon many, many times over. 1 Kings 11:1-3 says this,

"Now King Solomon loved many foreign women. Besides Pharaoh's daughter, he married women from Moab, Ammon, Edom, Sidon, and from among the Hittites. The Lord had clearly instructed the people of Israel, "You must not marry them, because they will turn your hearts to their gods." Yet Solomon insisted on loving them anyway. He had 700 wives of royal birth and 300 concubines. And in fact, they did turn his heart away from the Lord."

700 wives and 300 concubines add up to a pretty impressive number of women that had a sway on Solomon's heart. He may not have had Snapchat, tinder or access to pornography on his iPhone, but I think it's fair to say that the King had some sexual addictions that he masked with multiple marriages and concubines.

If you're married, you probably only have one wife (unless you live in Utah). But we need to look at the heart behind this command: prioritize and focus on the marriage you're in.

Even after 20 years of marriage, I am still realizing how much more I still have to work on my relationship with Rachel. It takes "intentionality" and work. My wife and I are leading a community group for married couples at church, using a video series from Jimmy Evans. It's amazing how I've been convicted about communication, and the nature of agape love, and how much *intentionality* a healthy marriage takes.

If you are single, you will never have an easier or better time to work on you, to work on your sexual integrity, and to work on your relationships. The Apostle Paul spoke of all the advantages of being single in the book of Corinthians (1 Corinthians 7:25-40). You can work on being a great husband way before you get married.

We could write an entire book, if not a library, on spiritual sons that lost everything because of sexual sin and indiscretion. If we could narrow down this principle to a rule, I would say this: **If we are going to be the spiritual sons that God has destined us to be, let's not neglect our marriages, and work on our sexual appetites to be fulfilled from our wives and our wives only.**

3. DON'T GET GREEDY.

"...nor shall he acquire for himself excessive silver and gold."

Another huge destiny-defeater and son-killer lies in the area of finances. We live in such an era of greed and materialism, that it can be too easy to let the desire for more resources and more things become a snare to us, drawing our hearts away from the Lord.

If we are going to be spiritual sons that finish strong we have to be those with godly perspectives and behaviors towards our finances.

Just as in marriage, we can always use a tune-up when it comes to finances. Here are three mindset shifts that will help us steward our finances well as spiritual sons:

a) What is your source of provision? *Even if you get a paycheck from a church, your source is always God, not the church budget, or senior pastor.*

b) Am I generous? *We have to constantly make sure we are generous and not clinging to what God has given us. My spiritual father always says, "Real giving starts after tithing!"*

c) Is money a tool I use, or does money make me a tool? (If you don't know what I mean, look up "tool" on Urban Dictionary). *We are the masters of our finances…our finances don't rule over us.*

4. STAY IN THE WORD.

"Also it shall be, when he sits on the throne of his Kingdom, that he shall write for himself a copy of this law in a book, from the one before the priests, the Levites. And it shall be with him, and he shall read it all the days of his life, that he may learn to fear the Lord his God and be careful to observe all the words of this law and these statutes, that his heart may not be lifted above his brethren, that he may not turn aside from the commandment to the right hand or to the left, and that he may prolong his days in his Kingdom, he and his children in the midst of Israel.

(Deuteronomy 17:18-20 NKJV)

The older I get, the more I want to know God and know about God. I want to study the Bible more and more, to understand Scripture on a deeper level. Like this passage says, we're blessed when we read and obey Scripture.

Unfortunately, as spiritual sons we can get so busy doing ministry that we forget about why we got into ministry in the first place—and we can neglect reading the Bible. It's key to keep spending time with God, diving into His Word, and keeping that fire for Him alive. If you need to get practical about it, get practical. Start a Bible reading plan, go on a fast, prayer walk, memorize new Scripture. Make your spiritual life a top priority again!

If we make these four benchmarks a priority, we will finish strong.

Remember,

1. Avoid anything that will take you back into bondage.
2. Full commitment to your one wife and sexual purity are crucial.
3. Examine your attitude towards finances. Are you in control of money, or is money in control of you?
4. Stay committed to reading and obeying Scripture.

We don't have to fizzle out like Solomon. We can actually get better with age…Jesus did!

And Jesus grew in wisdom and stature, and in favor with God and man.

(Luke 2:52)

Let's not be spiritual sons who start out great, but somewhere along the way, fall victim to the meaninglessness of life. Becoming a King or even taking over for our spiritual fathers is not enough. We can't just start the race well—we have to finish well.

In Paul's letter to his spiritual son Timothy, he says,

I have fought the good fight, I have finished the race, and I have remained faithful.

(2 Timothy 4:7)

Finishing well is a fight—and it's also a test of our character, our strength, and our trust in God. I can guarantee you there will be hurdles along the way to finishing the race. Temptations and trials will try to knock us off the path. But when we finish strong, we win.

CHAPTER THIRTEEN

PASSING ON THE SPIRITUAL DNA OF OUR FATHERS

For most of us, our spiritual fathers are men in ministry. They may lead churches, worship teams, or be overseers of church networks. We might even picture our own futures looking very similar to their lives. We might imagine ourselves speaking in front of crowds, writing bestselling books, and traveling all over the world to minister at mega churches. But the reality of life in ministry is that not all of us actually take over our spiritual fathers' specific work or Kingdom assignment.

Not all of us are called to be senior pastors, or head worship leaders, or apostles. Our callings might look different from those of our spiritual fathers. We might be called to be business professionals, teachers, artists, or even politicians, or we might have different roles in ministry.

Whether we are called to ministry, the marketplace, education, or another sphere of influence, we are *all* called to pass on the DNA of our spiritual fathers. We are all called to impart to others what has been imparted to us; to pass on the inheritance, the wisdom, and the blessing of having been a spiritual son, and to reach the next generation of sons who will change the world and advance the Kingdom of God.

In the case of the sons of David, one son stands out as passing on an incredible inheritance in the Kingdom of God.

Nathan never became the King of Israel. We never even hear his full life story, but unlike the sons of David who *didn't* leave their mark, Nathan left his mark on the history of humanity. We find his name again in the Bible, written thousands of years later in the book of Luke. He is mentioned in the direct lineage of Jesus—that's right, the seed of this "minor" son of David fathered the lineage of the Savior of the world.

Nathan is rarely talked about and probably never preached about, and is generally undervalued and ignored in the history of great men of God. And yet, this man had remarkable significance and made a lasting impact on history and humanity.

This unsung hero gives us insight on what true sonship is all about.

Nathan's story should teach us a lesson: we don't need a title and we don't need fanfare to accomplish great things for the Kingdom of God. We need to produce fruit that keeps on producing.

IT'S REALLY TRUE: EVERY PART OF THE BODY IS ESSENTIAL

The Apostle Paul said that "some parts of the body that seem weakest and least important are actually the most necessary" (1 Corinthians 12:22).

I'd never learned this lesson more than in my most recent season of building a church from the ground up in Los Angeles. My wife Rachel and I officially planted WaveChurch LA under the leadership of our senior pastors at WaveChurch Virginia Beach in 2014. We went from leading two campuses in North Carolina with a full staff, multiple volunteer teams, buildings with full facilities, and equipment to leading a church in our backyard with just a handful of people.

While leading a church and putting on Sunday service, it's the copy machines, sound techs, nursery care check-in, and parking lot attendants that may seem like the "little things"... until you don't have them anymore. But when you're trying to print out Sunday morning handouts, making sure the sound is functioning during worship, and facilitating parking all while preparing for your sermon, greeting people, and managing an entire team during Sunday morning, all of a sudden, the "details" don't seem like details anymore. They seem like essential cogs in the machine.

Likewise, when it comes to sonship, we often undervalue and fail to appreciate the most important characteristics of a man, a leader, and a son. It can be easy to glorify great charisma, presence, and reputation - especially in ministry - but it's often the people who support and serve others in hidden, unacknowledged ways that are the real heroes.

The "Nathan" of your church might be the guy who packs up the chairs after service, or who does behind-the-scenes work at the sound booth. Or, he might be the dad who's an incredible father, but who doesn't speak in front of crowds. And yet, he's reproducing fruit for the Kingdom of God. He's a pillar in the house of God, on which a lot will depend and be built.

SO, WHO *IS* NATHAN?

If you need to jog your memory on who Nathan actually *is* or where he is mentioned in Scripture, he is first mentioned in 2 Samuel 5:14-15:

> *These are the names of David's sons who were born in Jerusalem: Shammua, Shobab, Nathan, Solomon.*

Nathan was the third of four sons born to King David and Bathsheba. The first died as an infant; the last would become King Solomon—and Nathan was the third, the "middle child." But Nathan was significant, even at birth; in fact, he was the first one of Bathsheba's sons that she had the privilege of naming. And she named him after Nathan the prophet, her counselor and spiritual adviser. I guess she had big expectations for this little son.

And yet, we never really hear about Nathan again in the Old Testament. He seems overshadowed by both the accomplishments and mishaps of his brothers: Solomon, Adonijah, Absalom, Amnon, and others. But thousands of years later (and a few hundred pages in the Bible), his name appears again—in the gospel of Luke, which traces Jesus' lineage back to David through Nathan.

Jesus was known as the son of Joseph. Joseph was the son of Heli...Eliakim was the son of Melea. Melea was the son of Menna. Menna was the son of Mattatha. Mattatha was the son of Nathan. Nathan was the son of David.

(Luke 3:23, 31)

The gospel of Matthew, however, traces the lineage of Jesus back to David through Solomon, rather than Nathan (Matthew 1:6).

Some theologians even believe that *both* lineages are accurate. Any lineage written at the time would not have included maternal lineage, or lineage through a woman, leading some theologians to believe that Nathan can actually be traced to Jesus through Mary. Nathan could potentially have been the ancestor of Mary, and Solomon, the ancestor of Joseph. If we believe this is true, Nathan was an actual blood ancestor of Jesus.

This behind-the-scenes son was one of the most important sons of David. Although barely mentioned in Scripture, Nathan was responsible for prophetically carrying out the seed of David. His role was crucial to the greatest story ever told: the story of God sending His only son to the world to save humanity. Nathan might not have led a Kingdom, but he did bear fruit that lasted.

BEARING FRUIT THAT LASTS

Nathan's story lets us know that significance is not necessarily about fame, but about legacy. Ultimately, Nathan fulfilled the prophesies about Jesus in the Old Testament. The prophet Isaiah foretold that this would happen:

Out of the stump of David's family will grow a shoot—
yes, a new Branch bearing fruit from the old root.
And the Spirit of the LORD will rest on him—
the Spirit of wisdom and understanding,
the Spirit of counsel and might,
the Spirit of knowledge and the fear of the LORD.

(Isaiah 11:1-2)

The "new Branch" is Jesus, the Christ, the promised One. And Nathan helped bring this about by not just having a son of his own, but a son that would have another son, and so on.

The most important sons are not those that focus on their own success. The most world-changing, powerful sons are the ones that raise up others—who reproduce what they have been taught in others.

Sonship is not a one-man show about achieving singular fame. It's about reproducing the Kingdom.

We've got to grab hold of this truth: significance is found not in how many books we write, how many Twitter followers we get, how many church campuses we plant. It's in how we walk as spiritual sons—and how we produce other spiritual sons who understand these same principles. As a senior pastor and a spiritual father, one question I often ask myself is: *are my sons making it? Are my spiritual sons raising up more spiritual sons?* If the answer is "no," I know something is off-track, either in my own life or in their lives. I know that we've got to refocus and prioritize.

If this book helps a spiritual son stay on course, that's wonderful. But if it helps a spiritual son stay on course *and* causes him to raise up another son that also stays on course, then this book serves its purpose.

If I can raise both my birth son Silas and my spiritual sons to be spiritual fathers themselves, I will have a lineage that eventually, like Nathan's, will see the ushering and returning of the Lord. I won't just be a quick blip on the screen—I'll have made a significant contribution to raising up the Church in the last days.

Our purpose is always to produce a harvest:

"The seed that fell on good soil represents those who truly hear and understand God's word and produce a harvest of thirty, sixty, or even a hundred times as much as had been planted!"
(Matthew 13:23)

In 1 Kings 4:5 it states "Azariah **son of Nathan**—in charge of the district governors" when listing the chief officials of Israel under the reign of Solomon.

The passage does not specify if Azariah is the son of Nathan the prophet or Nathan the son of David. But could it be that Nathan, David's son was remarkable at developing spiritual sons? Not only Mattatha (mentioned in the lineage in Luke), but maybe also Azariah?

As we've seen in the previous chapters, it's one thing to *become* a son—it's another thing to sustain sonship, especially sonship that will reproduce. In order to avoid the pitfalls that may take us out of reproducing fruitfulness, there are certain principles to keep in mind:

Here are five ways to keep the legacy going....

1. DON'T LET THE DRAMA TAKE YOU OUT.

Notice that all the stories of sons that end in failure- Amnon's, Absalom's, Adonijah's and Solomon's- are filled with unnecessary drama. We may not be able to control everything around us, but we can be intentional and avoid useless conflict, temptation, gossip, and manipulation that come with people in your life who thrive on dysfunction.

If it's the case that you feel surrounded by drama, even in church, I'm *sorry*... but don't allow yourself to fall into the same trap! Not once in the sometimes chaotic and relationally "complicated" life of David do we hear about Nathan getting involved with any of the issues of his brothers. Whether that was coincidental or intentional on the part of Nathan, follow his example of staying removed from unnecessary drama, and finish the race strong.

2. BE GENEROUS IN EVERY ARENA.

Nathan can be translated to mean "to give." I believe there are a lot of young men reading this book today whom I've been generous to in the past. It could have been with finances, with support through a difficult time, help on a church-planting team, or even graphic design for their ministry. I believe that by giving generously we actually guarantee that our legacy will continue.

Proverbs 11:24-26 says,

The world of the generous gets larger and larger and the world of the stingy gets smaller and smaller. (MSG)

3. UNDERSTAND EVERYONE IS REPLACEABLE

Ouch. This sounds harsh, but thinking we are irreplaceable will only set us up for failure. When a man abdicates his call from God, God will put another man in his place. David replaced Saul, and, in a sense, when Solomon backslid from God, Nathan took his place as the Davidic seed to the Messiah. God always had a replacement plan. I don't think we should live in fear, but we need to know that there's a standard to which God holds us.

When we miss it, we can be replaced by someone else. We should be reminded that it is by God's grace we were made new creations, and by God's grace that we will continue in Christ.

In 1 Kings 19, Elijah thought he was the only man of God left (verse 14), and God said he had 7000 in reserve (verse 18). It's humbling to know that if we mess up, God can and will continue His work….with or without us!

4. YOU DON'T NEED A TITLE.

Isn't it amazing that Nathan's greatest accomplishment for the Kingdom of God was not even known by his own generation? He didn't appear to have any titles, or have special recognition in the Kingdom of Israel. And yet in the eternal Kingdom of God, he will go down as a father in the lineage of Jesus.

If we are title-driven in our efforts for the Kingdom of God, we can suffer a lot of letdown and disappointment when we don't get the position or title that we aimed for. We can pastor without the title of Pastor, or be an Elder without a special reserved parking spot. You can be a person of influence even if you only have 213 followers on Instagram. The most important and transformational thing we can ever do as ministers of the gospel is to love people and help them grow in their relationship with God. Be a pillar in God's house with your consistency, wisdom and support.

Influence those around you, even if it's just one person. In the case of Nathan, we only know for sure that he influenced his son Mattatha... but that one case eventually birthed our Messiah.

5. DON'T GET CAUGHT IN THE" I DESERVE" LIE OF THE ENEMY

You know now that Nathan was actually Solomon's older brother. How would you like the Queen of Sheba to come to your little brother, so impressed with his wisdom? When Solomon was being praised, there were probably some moments where Nathan could have thrown him under the bus. I imagine Nathan thinking, *Oh, yeah? Remember the time when he lost the camel, put a whoopee cushion under Mephishobeth's chair, married a crazy lady, or got busted TP-ing the city gates?*

The point is we don't ever hear of Nathan trying to usurp Solomon's authority by using his older brother card. And because he didn't, he made history.

I've seen too many sons miss out on their destiny because they fell for the trap of "I deserve this." In all honesty, we don't really want what we deserve—we deserve the judgment of God, but we want grace. Leave a legacy by His grace, and not by what you may think you deserve.

Nathan, the son of David, reminds us all about what it is to be a true spiritual son. It's not about titles, recognition or even what we think we deserve. Being a Son is about creating a legacy that will birth the coming back of our Savior Jesus.

This chapter is about putting our perspective on value and significance back where it belongs: in bearing fruit for the Kingdom, specifically fruit that reproduces. Jesus described producing a harvest this way:

The seed that fell on good soil represents those who truly hear and understand God's word and **produce a harvest of thirty, sixty, or even a hundred times as much as had been planted!**

(Matthew 13:23)

Passing on the spiritual DNA of our fathers means that we reproduce fruit that lasts.

CHAPTER FOURTEEN

SON OF DAVID

So far, we've read about a son who raped his own sister, a son who committed serial homicide, a son who tried to promote himself to King of Israel, a son who died as an infant because of his father's sin, multiple sons who completely missed their destinies, and a son with all the potential in the world, who turned from God and allowed a Kingdom with great worth and destiny to disintegrate.

In most of the stories we've read about and learned from we see sons that have been disqualified from the running because of their own sins, mistakes, and shortcomings.

I certainly have felt like one of the disqualified sons at different points of my life.

When my dad died, I lost my pastor, my coach, my disciplinarian, my goofy best friend and most importantly, my father. I was only 16. I didn't immediately react in an unhealthy way, but about three years after his death, I lashed out. Influenced by a dangerous combo of adolescence and grief, I struck out on a messy trail of self-sabotage. I had always been a very good kid. I respected my parents, stayed out of trouble, and obeyed the rules I had been taught. But in the span of months- if not weeks- I did all the things my Father had raised me not to do. I stole from my work and my grieving mother, I partied, I lied, I manipulated the people closest to me. I had become completely out of control.

You've already read this story in Chapter One, so you know the details: how I was restored back to sonship, how I'm still learning to be the son that God has called me to be. And if it weren't for *the* Son, I'd probably still be as lost as I was as an angry, disobedient 19-year old.

Being a spiritual son means that a lot stands on your shoulders—not only your own future, but the future of a whole generation of spiritual sons that you may be called to raise up to further advance the Kingdom of God.

Are you hearing me? Your future is *incredible*…you are going to transform lives everywhere you go with the authority, power, and love that God has given you through the power of the Holy Spirit.

That's exactly why the enemy will try to take you down.

In John 10:10, Jesus says, "The thief's purpose is to steal and kill and destroy."

The enemy would love to attack and destroy spiritual sons because he knows that if they fall, the Kingdom will fall. God will still stand sovereign, but the failure of sons to fulfill their destinies means that countless lives will be lost from the Kingdom of God.

ISRAEL: A DESTINY THWARTED, BUT NOT DESTROYED

In the story of David and his sons (and his sons' sons), we see conflict and division succeeding in taking down destinies. Instead of continuing to unite the Kingdom of Israel, built and strengthened under the leadership of his grandfather David, Solomon's Son Rehoboam actually divided Israel, setting it up for future decline and destruction. The people of Israel asked King Rehoboam to lighten the labor demands and heavy taxes imposed by his father—and when he refused, this was their response:

When all Israel realized that the King had refused to listen to them, they responded,

"Down with the dynasty of David!
We have no interest in the son of Jesse.

Back to your homes, O Israel!

Look out for your own house, O David!"

(1 Kings 12:16)

In the case of the Kingdom of Israel, the enemy had won, at least for a time. They were divided, they fell, and they momentarily lost their destiny. This was a painful era for Israel: they were eventually ruled over by the Babylonians, Assyrians and Romans, temples destroyed, cities sieged, experiencing 400-plus years of repression.

Thank God for His promises and His unrelenting determination to restore His people.

There was a glimmer of hope during the chaos and the tragedy. During the split of Israel and in the hundreds of years after, a prophecy was spoken that promised to restore and redeem the house of David, the temple of God, and the Kingdom of Israel. And this would be a restoration to a greater degree of glory than David or any of his sons or grandsons could ever have imagined.

When David died, God delivered His Word to David through the prophet Nathan:

For when you die and are buried with your ancestors, I will raise up one of your descendants, your own offspring, and I will make his Kingdom strong. He is the one who will build a house—a temple—for my name. And I will secure his royal throne forever.

(2 Samuel 7:12-13)

And then, hundreds of years later, the prophet Jeremiah came onto the scene during a time of great turmoil and disobedience. At this time, Israel had turned away from God completely, and was under the rule of the Babylonians. But Jeremiah wasn't all doom and gloom. He gave them hope, prophecying to the people:

Behold, the days are coming," says the LORD, "That I will raise to David a Branch of righteousness; a King shall reign and prosper, and execute judgment and righteousness in the earth. In His days Judah will be saved, and Israel will dwell safely; now this is His name by which He will be called: THE LORD OUR RIGHTEOUSNESS.

(Jeremiah 23:5-6 NKJV)

A Son was promised to the nation of Israel, One that would not self-sabotage, and would reign on the throne—forever. This is a Son who would never disappoint, screw up, or wreck His destiny.

ENTER *THE* SON OF THE PROMISE

Jesus, the Son of God, was also called the Son of David. That's right—the Son of God was also called the Son of a man who fell hard into sexual sin, and who made mistake after mistake with his own kids.

But in order to fulfill the prophecy that would mean restoration and redemption for Israel and for all nations, Jesus came to the world as one of David's very own offspring.

In fact, the very first sentence of the gospel of Matthew calls Jesus the "Son of David" (Matthew 1:1). And then throughout the gospels, we hear this term again and again—Jesus is called "Son of David" by the writers of the gospels, the people He heals, and the crowds who gather around Him.

Many called Jesus the "Son of David." But we're going to focus on one man in particular, whom many theologians believe to be the first man who publicly acknowledged Jesus with this title. This guy recognized that this Jewish Rabbi was the One who would reign on the throne forever and forever, build a house that would never fall, and rule with perfect justice…and he couldn't even *see* him.

The story of blind Bartimeaus comes 14 generations, or about 490 years, after the shortcomings of David's immediate sons: after Amnon's rape of his sister, Absalom's rebellion, Adonijah's self-promotion, Solomon's wisdom lost, and all the other sons with lost and failed destinies.

Mark 10 tells the story this way:

Then they reached Jericho, and as Jesus and his disciples left town, a large crowd followed him. A blind beggar named

Bartimaeus (son of Timaeus) was sitting beside the road. When Bartimaeus heard that Jesus of Nazareth was nearby, he began to shout, "Jesus, Son of David, have mercy on me!"

"Be quiet!" many of the people yelled at him.

But he only shouted louder, "Son of David, have mercy on me!"

When Jesus heard him, he stopped and said, "Tell him to come here."

So they called the blind man. "Cheer up," they said. "Come on, he's calling you!" Bartimaeus threw aside his coat, jumped up, and came to Jesus.

"What do you want me to do for you?" Jesus asked.

"My Rabbi," the blind man said, "I want to see!"

And Jesus said to him, "Go, for your faith has healed you." Instantly the man could see, and he followed Jesus down the road.

(Mark 10:46-52)

Somewhere just outside Jericho, whose walls once tried to impede God's people from possessing their Promised Land, a declaration was made that shook history. This blind beggar announced and declared that Jesus from Nazerene was not just the son of a carpenter, but the Son of David.

Son of David, have mercy on me.

This is the fulfillment of prophecies and prayers: finally, David had a Son that was worthy of the Kingdom of Israel and worthy to be King of the world, a Son that can teach us true sonship. Since the centuries that followed the reign and rule of David, there had been many sons, but only one was qualified to be called the Son of David. All the other sons had disqualified themselves.

There are a few key principles we can learn from this story of one son who saw another Son—and felt hope.

1. JESUS BREAKS CYCLES OF SICKNESS, SIN, AND BROKENNESS.

Some theologians believe when you translate the name of Bartimaeus, it means "blind son of a blind father."* But his faith in

Jesus healed him, breaking a generational cycle of blindness in his family.

No matter how much you've screwed up as a son, or if you've repeated the sinful or unhealthy patterns you've seen in your own father, Jesus can help you break the cycles of sin, shame, pain, and disappointment in your life. It starts with recognizing who He is: the One that restores all things.

2. A REVELATION OF JESUS AS THE SON OF DAVID WILL CHANGE THE WAY YOU SEE THINGS.

Bartimaeus came to his spot on the side of the road that day completely blind, and after one encounter with Jesus, he left seeing and knowing himself as a son. Because he saw in the spiritual what he could not see in the natural, his sight was restored to him. Bartimaeus had revelation that Jesus was the Son of David, and everything else fell into place: his physical healing, his identity in Christ, and his identity as a son.

When we get a true revelation that Jesus is the Messiah, the Son of David, it causes us to see who we are in Christ and our destiny in the Kingdom of God. Bartimaeus hadn't heard anyone else call Jesus "Son of David." This was a fresh and prophetic insight coming from a man who hadn't been worthy of much at all in the eyes of the world… until he became one of the original heralds of the Messiah.

Christian counselors can be extremely valuable, but one of the most transformative things we can ever experience is special revelation from God that opens our eyes to see things the way God sees them. I believe that revelation from the Holy Spirit can do more than a thousand counseling appointments, by causing us to see ourselves and others better and clearer through the lens of God.

3. WHEN YOU ANNOUNCE JESUS FOR WHO HE IS, PEOPLE WILL WANT TO QUIET YOU DOWN.

All Bartimaeus wanted to do was get healed, yet even the crowd that was following Jesus wanted him to stay quiet. In a sense, they wanted him to just stick to being blind—his yelling out towards Jesus was causing a lot of unwanted drama, chaos, and attention.

Don't let people quiet you on your quest for healing. Be a man who cries out to Jesus for complete emotional and physical healing, so you can be the son that God calls you to be: fully restored and delivered.

4. KEEP YELLING.

I love Bartimaeus' determination to only yell all the more when the crowd was trying to shut him up. He didn't just yell more; he yelled *louder*. He wasn't going to scale down his efforts to get Jesus' attention because of shame or embarrassment. He had been blind his entire life, and was determined to get healed.

We all have to be determined that one way or another, we will be healed of whatever is weighing us down or hindering us from destiny: sickness, sin strongholds, past hurts and pain, and unforgiveness.

Remember that all of creation is waiting for the manifestation of the Sons of God. If we don't get healed and become the sons God has called us to be…then creation continues to wait.

5. HE'S CALLING YOU.

Jesus tells Bartimaeus to come to Him—"Cheer up," they said. "Come on, he's calling you!"

Jesus was asking Bartimaeus to come near to Him. When Jesus speaks, His words empower—Bartimaeus got up, drew near to Jesus, and was healed. The One who lives in you (2 Corinthians 13:5) is also calling you to a greater purpose. And when He calls, He qualifies you to do just what He has asked of you.

The crowd around Bartimaeus told him to cheer up. They knew that the One calling this blind man would give him the ability to do just what He has asked. The greatest joy is to know that Jesus is not only calling us, He's empowering us to be sons that advance the Kingdom.

6. THROW DOWN YOUR CLOAK.

When Bartimaeus threw down his cloak, he signified that he was willing to throw away his current identity to get a better one. Whether that coat was a coat that signified to others he was blind, or the coat was something worth value, he regarded it as useless in that moment. When it came to healing, Bart didn't allow anything to keep him to his past. He threw down his coat to get ready for his future.

What things can we release right now so that we will be ready to be sons? Stepping into new identity may mean that you release old parts of your identity, even parts that you might see as valuable or necessary.

7. BARTIMAEUS KNEW WHAT HE NEEDED, AND WHAT HE WANTED.

Jesus asked Bartimaeus, "What do you want me to do for you?" although it would have been obvious to him that Bartimaeus was blind. But Jesus wanted him to say exactly what he wanted, and what he needed.

I hope this book has helped you identify specific issues you may be experiencing with sonship. Be specific when you ask to be healed in those areas. Jesus wants to hear you tell Him exactly what it is that you want: *Son of David, would you heal me in my resentment against my pastor who did me wrong? Jesus, would you heal me of lust in my thought life? Son of David, would you heal me of my forgiveness?*

8. GET HEALED AND DELIVERED. THEN KEEP FOLLOWING JESUS.

After Bartimaeus is healed, he follows Jesus. First, he called him" the Son of David"—then he called him "Rabbi".

If we are truly going to be great sons, we have to be willing for Jesus to teach us, and we have to be willing to follow Him, wherever He might lead us. What plan do you have to continue on the path to following Jesus? How are you going to let him be your Rabbi, your teacher?

9. YOUR "FAITH HAS HEALED YOU."

Jesus said to Bartimaeus that his faith had healed him. Imagine a lifetime of struggle, years of shame, unable to work or even function well in society, all healed in an instant. Bartimaeus believed in Jesus and in His love, His mercy, His power to heal. And it transformed his life forever; in fact, it gave him an entirely new life.

No doubt great challenges and difficulties will come our way and try to derail us from our destiny in God. It's going to take faith to be a son of the promise, faith to stay on course, faith to apprehend our destiny, faith to leave our mark on the world, faith to be healed of our past, and faith to master the art of sonship.

A LOST ART, RECOVERED

In closing, the lost art of sonship doesn't have to be lost anymore. My heart is for this generation to recover sonship, to step into destiny that is never derailed.

We can begin to heal from our past, break vicious cycles in our lives, and become sons that will raise up the sons that all of creation is waiting for. It won't always be easy. In fact, most of the time it won't be easy. Sometimes, we will have to choose not to be ruled by our emotions. We will have to choose not to get offended, even when we're hurt. We will have to constantly remind ourselves of the foundations laid for us and of who we are in Christ.

But if we do, we will reign with the Son of David!

Can I pray with you?

Jesus, Son of David, have mercy on me. I know you've called me to be a son. I want to honor my spiritual fathers. I want continue to build on their legacy. More importantly, I realize that when I understand sonship, it helps me in my relationship with my heavenly Father. Jesus, because I am joint heirs with you, I can also be a son of David and help rule and reign in this Kingdom and the Kingdom to come.

Holy Spirit, heal me where I need to be healed. Father God, I ask for forgiveness where I've not forgiven. Jesus help me not to stay offended. Help me be a son that by not self-sabotaging his destiny, will actually pick up my spiritual father's mantle at the appropriate time, and help accomplish the things he did and even more.

Help me be a son that all of creation is waiting for.

In Jesus' name, Amen.

*Mark 10, The Pulpit Commentaries

Moore, George F. "Fourteen Generations: 490 Years: An Explanation of the Genealogy of Jesus" *The Harvard Theological Review* http://www.jstor.org/stable/1507663

VISIT

ISRAELCAMPBELL.COM

to learn more
about the author